Excerpts from Infinity

Swami Jnananandaji and Dharma

DEDICATION

To Dharma, the dog who was not a dog, and to unknown saints everywhere. May their light illuminate our hearts.

INTRODUCTION

All things come from One source. That source is Infinite, and from that Infinity comes the tremendous diversity of life. Everything is expressing differently as the One light.

While all things are breathing and living that Presence, there are beings whose words and breath are the fragrance of that Living Presence.

They seem to speak, listen, and breathe on behalf of Infinity. They stretch the definition of what a human being can be far beyond the imagination of what might be possible. They defy gravity!

My dear friend and teacher, what words could ever convey how my life changed forever in your energetic embrace?

When we first met He asked me to write down the stories He shared with me.

"I am not good at remembering these sorts of things," I replied.

"I will help you remember," He replied.

I have pondered those words: "I will help you remember." Unquestionably, there was often a grace in remembering stories and events from our times together, but, more than that, it seems like it sums up the entirety of our relationship, which was one pointed towards helping me to remember the Divine Self that dwells in the hearts of All.

Over the next ten years, I would visit several times a year, and gradually the stack of journals I was writing in grew in size. I later consolidated them into a book and presented them to Swami Jnanananda. He was kind enough to read them and check them for accuracy and make a few corrections.[1]

Sitting in the little room where He gave satsang, I was often overwhelmed with gratitude. For here was a man who wanted nothing from the world, but offered freely more love, wisdom, light, and joy than I had ever seen in one human being.

It is my humble hope that a small portion of that love and wisdom spill over from these journals and into the heart of the reader. Truly the journals are a labor of love.

Devdas (aka Steve) and Swami Jnananandaji (aka Maharaj)

The stories are presented chronologically and, thus, in a certain sense, the book starts out slow and shows something of my own transformation over the years.

---

[1] Probably the last 10 or so stories in the journal were not checked by the saint.

It may help the flow and understanding of these stories to share a few sentences about my own story, since it is interwoven in places into the narrative:

When I first came to India I was a Brahmachari[2] in the tradition of kriya yoga.[3] Kriya yoga was popularized by the Indian saint Paramhansa Yogananda, whom many people know from his famous book *Autobiography of a Yogi*.

After almost six years of monastic life, it seemed like it was time for a new direction. By Grace, I then met Sumakshi Singh. Sumakshi and I often went to Dehradun together, and when Jnananandaji read this journal He said He could feel her presence in it as well. Indeed it is true that this book would not be the same without her, and I am supremely grateful both for her and for her contribution to this book.

Sumakshi Singh with Swami Jnananandaji

---

[2] The first stage in monastic life.

[3] Sri Jnananandaji also came from the tradition of kriya yoga, although from a slightly different lineage. His Guru was Swami Atmananandaji, which is covered in more detail in the journals.

Visiting Jnanananda usually consisted of chai and biscuits, then kirtan,[4] and then prasad.[5] Most of the stories happened over chai, as is the custom with sadhus.[6]

What a gift to be given the opportunity to sit with someone who lives as a pure reflection of the One Light. That Living Presence is the Presence of love, peace, and joy in depth beyond imagination. May these stories transport the seeker into the heart of Infinite Love and give a taste of the Living Presence.

Devdas

---

[4] Kirtan is devotional singing, in this case with the accompaniment of a harmonium.

[5] Prasad is usually Indian sweets, offered to the Divine and then shared amongst people in attendance.

[6] A sadhu is someone who wanders, heart attuned to the Divine. Maharaj spent most of His life as a wandering sadhu.

A Jewish devotee came to celebrate God's leela[7] in the Himalayas. He mentioned that, as a Jew, he was used to God without form, and yet on his journey in India he beheld a statue of the Goddess. Above the Goddess a door opened—a portal really—into another world more bright, more alive, more full.

Remember: every God, every Goddess, is a window into another world, into and beyond this Maya.[8]

****

So many stories Jnananandaji told about Jews. Like the young Jewish man who meditated for ten days on the sound of the Ganges, even without the suggestion of Jnanananda (who loved to suggest exactly this to the lovers of Ma Ganga).

Certainly I, myself, was Jewish in a past life. Is exile so bad? We are all in exile. Jnananandaji used to say that we are all orphans. We perceive ourselves to be separate from the One source. We look outward for satisfaction, when the greatest joy lies inside.

****

The banks of the great river Narmada are filled with semiprecious stones. When you walk in the moonlight, you can see them sparkle.

---

[7] Leela means "Divine Play." Often used to refer to the lives of saints, like Ramakrishna's leela.

[8] Maya literally means "illusion," referring to the dream of God, but it can also be translated as "miracle," because life in its astounding diversity is miraculous.

Jnananandaji's Shiva lingam came from the same river. Ram's picture adorns the rock, as does the head of the tortoise that carries the Universe. The circumference of the Shiva lingam makes a zero. Look at it the other way and it forms a dot, symbolizing infinity.

When Sri Jnanananda was wandering, He met a saint. They sat in a small room until the saint leaned forward and asked if Sri Jnanananda would like to see Maya.

"I was young then," Mahatmaji said with a twinkle in His eye, "and perhaps a little foolish, so I said yes. In any case," He added, "Sanyasis[9] are meant to have no fear."

The saint then pulled the cover off of a small table, and inside was a Shiva lingam surrounded by mirrors. There were slits in the side of the table where you could look in. Inside, the Shiva lingam was reflected an infinite number of times.

Infinity... caught in many forms, each one forgetting for a time that it is, indeed, the Infinite.

****

"Do you believe that when you do kriya, Babaji's[10] blessing is with you?" the Mahatma asked one day in satsang.

_____

[9] A sanyasi is one who has renounced the world in search of the true Self. The verb form of the same word is "sanyas," so in the case of Jnanananda, He received His sanyas from Atmananda, His teacher and guide, and that made Him a sanyasi.

[10] Babaji is the Great Deathless Avatar mentioned in Yogananda's book *Autobiography of a Yogi*. Kriya is a form of pranayam

"Yes," I replied.

"Do you think Babaji can give just His blessing?" Mahatmaji paused for a moment and then added, "He cannot."

Slowly with a pause in between each word He uttered, "He...is...with...you."

My whole being shivered with joy, and I knew that what He said was true.

****

"I knew a devotee," said Jnananandaji, "who opened his heart to Babaji and said, 'Oh Babaji, how can I do this kriya? Come please and show me.' Then the kriyas started by themselves."

"But when the man left the meditation, the kriyas did not stop." Kriya in the office, kriya at home. This kind of thing is possible, if you are receptive and open.

****

Sri Jnanananda's Guru, Atmananandaji, was at a funeral once, for a man that he had not known that well. The man's wife approached him and asked if Sri Atmananandaji would help her in the process of leaving the body with higher kriya. She wanted someone to be there and to help her.

---

reintroduced to the world, mainly by Yogananda, through the same book.

She had taken her diksha[11] from another Guru, one of Lahiri's disciples, and yet Atmanandaji felt to accept this somewhat strange request.

Later they met and sat to meditate. Atmanandaji was highly advanced, and he could see her astral and causal bodies working, and he then witnessed all her prana go to the spiritual eye, then to the thousand petaled lotus, and then she left the body.

A few minutes later the body was "dead," as the soul had departed.

****

When asked to give a lecture on aging, Jnanananda, as usual, took a slightly different approach.

"Each of us carefully records the slow process of our 'getting old' by marking birthdays with gifts and celebration. Yet each of us has been born thousands of times. In addition, every cell in our body is replaced every fifteen years, so the soul outlives the body even in this lifetime."

The Mahatma then asked His listeners the simple question: "Why, then, do we age?"

****

Jnananandaji's poem, "The Individual," cured a woman of cancer.

The Mahatma said she was sitting in the hospital, and she would write it over and over again. Eventually she wrote it out in beautiful calligraphy and sent it to

---

[11] Diksha is "initiation" by a guru.

Mahatmaji. Later, He added a drawing (which someone else had drawn) to the top, and He often gave this to new people who were coming to satsang.

THE INDIVIDUAL

Ideals —
  Divine ideals!
The secret treasures
  of man's youth.
Life's love and wisdom,
  fragrant recollections
of by-gone times
  in former lives.
At present
  they reflect
the light
  of the soul.
Oh Ideal
  Aspiration!
When heart expands
  and feelings flood
  one's entire being,
Thought tries
  to capture —
    grasp —
the all-eluding One
  in a readiness
to sacrifice
  the little Self.
Being One
  with God
in the heart
  of all!
Oh Friend Divine,
  Thy sacred touch
Awakens memories,
  intuitions sweet
of a relationship
  with the most High.
At heart — thou art
When heart is one and only!
No more a stranger
  in this world,
But self-illumined
  by his greater Self,
He dwells
  and has his being
in the Soul of all!
Humanity —
  on cross-roads
Of diversities
  betwixt light
and intense darkness.
Where senses mighty,
  lamps and shades,
Conjure up a magic show of Unreality…
  assuming countless
Names and shapes

in endless, limitless
Dimensions —
  expanding wide,
Wider, faster still, into immense
  proportions
in time and space
  of man's own fancy!
Thus lost
  in the confusion
of his own creations
  man fails to find his Soul ;
man fails
  to claim his truly Own —
    The Whole!
A world made whole
  by God,
for him alone.
  Not that he should
divide it and possess its parts,
  but that he would share it whole
with Himself
  in all!
Oh my Beloved
  Child of God.
Awake —
  Arise —
and claim
  the whole of
Thy inheritance Divine!
Each one a
  Master — King
Servant — Lover !
  One in all,
In whom
  the Whole
remains
  forever,
an undisturbed
  undivided
    Whole
For God Eternal
  is whole;
His Creation Divine
  is whole;
and whole is man
  as Son of God.
He is poised
  in Peace,
At rest,
  undivided
within Himself!

  Aum

Jnanananda hitchhiked from Europe to India over three months. He knew nobody. He told His friends and loved ones that they would not hear from Him for 12 years.

When He finally got to the border of India, there was a Sardar border guard who was quite tall and ominous looking. He asked Sri Jnanananda the simple question, "Why have you come to India?" The Mahatma had an equally simple answer. He said, "To find God."

The guard then countered and asked, "Do you have a Guru?"

Mahatmaji replied, "Yes."

That ominous border guard then smiled and said simply, "Welcome to India!"

Once here, Sri Jnanananda would spend six months with Atmananandaji at Dakshineswar[12] (Yogoda Math) and then six months as a sadhu living with Swamis in mud huts made with bamboo, mud, and pine needle roofs. Of course this was not an exact schedule, it was a flow of Divine Grace where Mahatmaji listened inwardly for guidance where and when to move.

Those huts that the Mahatma lived in are, to this day, unoccupied. Divine Mother is saving them for a soul with great courage and the sincere desire to know God.

****

---

[12] Dakshineswar is just outside Kolkata, where the famous Indian Master Ramakrishna had his leela.

The Mahatma said once simply:

Every birth is your birth, every death is your death.

＊＊＊＊＊＊＊＊＊＊＊＊＊＊＊＊

Jnananandaji can see the Oneness and share it. This is not a mere thought. It is experience.

Saints do not come to tell you how great they are, they come to tell us who and what we are. Jnananandaji is a perfect mirror. In His Presence I can feel, if only for a moment, that I, too, am all that He is.

＊＊＊＊＊＊＊＊＊＊＊＊＊＊＊＊

Jnanananda showed us a photo of a yogi who had burned himself from the inside out with his internal yogic fire. The photo displayed a radiant face of joy and peace and a charred body underneath. The fire had even burned the bed that this yogi was laying on.

Another woman burned for ten days while still conscious. No embers that were added to the fire would burn, because hers was an inner fire.

Coincidentally, at this time, Jemal[13] and I had been doing long maha mudra sessions—a technique which can generate a lot of heat in the body. Jnanananda reached out with His hand and said not to worry. The inner fire will only bring you beatitude, only peace.

＊＊＊＊＊＊＊＊＊＊＊＊＊＊＊＊

---

[13] Jemal was the head monk in the monastery I was a part of. He is still a monk living in India in charge of a monastery. A very beautiful soul and a dear friend.

All life is conscious—even the air and the space in between.

Jemal and I had been pondering this thought on our pilgrimage, and when we got to Sri Jnanananda's, He picked up the thought. "Most people look at things," the Mahatma said, "but they are not trained to look in between. How many people ask what is between you and I? Even the space between is conscious."

The Mahatma then shared a story from the life of Anandamayi Ma, a great saint of India. Ma was once crowded by people seeking her darshan,[14] and a devotee who was standing near her was worried about the cramped quarters and thinking perhaps Ma would be claustrophobic. Ma caught the thought and simply said, "I am this body, I am those bodies, and I am all the space in between."

At the Kumba Mela with the ashram of Anandamayi Ma (From left: unknown, Steve, Devendra, unknown, Jaidhara, Jemal)

---

[14] Darshan is a Sanskrit word from the root dṛś, which means "to see." In this case, the sight or blessing of a holy person or saint.

****

Jnanananda knew a doctor who learned to heal himself by God's power, but he still saw patients and offered prescriptions, sometimes for free.

That doctor, much like the Mahatma Himself, knew that you have to work with people where they are.

****

Jemal and I arrived after several days in Lakshman Jhula. It was as if Jnananandaji had been there with us the whole time.

As Jemal and I had been traveling, we had been talking about God and about the spiritual path, and when we reached the Mahatma, He simply answered every question that we had been discussing, without us even having to ask.

Jemal had wanted to know the location of secret caves in the area, and so Mahatmaji talked with us at length about the secret caves in the area and where to find them. I had been talking about the Mahatma's song Ananda Brahma, which He played a very long and beautiful version of.

When you recognize that you are one with everything, think how much you can help your Self. All our thoughts were His thoughts, because, to Him, there is no difference between ourselves and Himself, because it is only a reflection of God. And in His presence, one could not help but feel that was the Truth.

****

On that same journey, Jnanananda said to Jemal and I:

You worked hard in the past, and that is why you are where you are now. Of course you have always been the same, and yet there is an unfolding of the soul.

****

In a moment of clarity, Jemal once turned to me in a hotel room and simply said, "Babaji is holding this all together with his mind."

That simple sentence was said with the power of Truth behind it. As such, it penetrated deeply.

Everything is breathing. Not just the air, but the energy going up and down that causes the breath. Even Babaji's trident has a breath. Up and down the spine. Everything in the cosmos is breathing, and breath itself is the song of creation.

Be thankful for each breath.

A Mohammedan once told Jnananandaji to be thankful for the inhale, and to be thankful for the exhale. Mahatmaji then added that He should also be thankful for the space in between the breaths—when there is no movement at all.

****

Jnananandaji once knew a man who bathed after someone stepped on his shadow. Mahatmaji told this story with a laugh, indicating that people can take things too far.

Sometimes, yogis who are quite conscious of energy and magnetism become too aware, and they estrange themselves from the people around them who are, of course, manifestations of the One.

****

Jnananandaji used to always ask people if they came in a car with a driver. If they did He would wrap up some prasad to take out to the driver.

This, of course, is not that noteworthy, but it is wonderful to see that each one of us is cared for, and nobody excluded from the Infinite love.

****

There is a secret society of Switzerland and India. Somewhere near the Ganges there is a portal. Look for the ashram M. nagar—near there you may find answers.

****

A man from Switzerland left for the mountains on a 20-year journey. He brought no food. Later, he wrote the constitution of Switzerland: always neutral, neither left nor right.

Some of his descendants came to Rishikesh, and they were hypnotists. When they came, they left hypnotism behind. Light psychic powers ran in the family, and even the little boy could see auras. "Mommy, why is that person green?" he would ask. Or, "Why does that tree have an aura?"

At this point in the story Mahatmaji shifted gears and asked a question, "Do you know who is most susceptible to being hypnotized?"

There was a moment of silence before He answered.

"The person who strongly thinks that he cannot be hypnotized is the most susceptible."

Most people walking around in delusion are not even aware they are characters in the dream of God. Anyone who knows this, has tremendous respect for the power of the dream. Ultimately, it is grace that wakes up the dreamer from the delusion of separateness.

****

"Everything is in the scriptures of India. Everything from space travel to the inward journey—but you need a Guru to be able to understand it!"

****

Everyone who comes asks for a blessing. Some get a little bit, and some get more. One night, Mahatmaji shared His thoughts on this with a story.

"Once, a group of rishis sat pondering the question of how to get more of God's grace. Kripa means 'grace.' It is always with us."

The Mahatma then commented on the discovery by saying, "What draws grace is grace."

****

Jnananandaji, when He was a young man, had absolutely the best kind of visa for India. He had befriended someone high up in the Indian government, and they asked him, "What kind of visa do you want?"

He replied, "Why don't you tell me what kind is best?"

During that time, many Western sadhus and monks were forced out of India for visa reasons, but Jnananandaji was safe. One policeman actually said, "No one can touch Jnanananda."

How could they touch Him when He is One with everything?

✳✳✳✳✳✳✳✳✳✳✳✳✳✳✳✳

Mahatmaji sometimes spoke in riddles. One day:

"It is not enough to eat, you must also be a good cook. But some people do not even know how to eat!"

✳✳✳✳✳✳✳✳✳✳✳✳✳✳✳✳

From my personal diary after a visit to Mahatmaji:

How few people understand the incredible gift that is a saint. How can anyone give enough thanks for sitting in a room with a pure expression of the One?

✳✳✳✳✳✳✳✳✳✳✳✳✳✳✳✳

The Mahatma was not above a good laugh, one day He ventured,"Why do Hindu gods have so many arms?"

Then with great amusement He replied, "So they can talk on the cell phone!"

****

Swami Dhirananda from SRF[15] came to visit Sri Jnanananda with an old man who had been a big donor to SRF and also to the Ramakrishna Order.

The man was suffering from some illness and asked Jnanananda what kind of yoga he could do to help his recovery.

"Have you ever seen a child," Jnananandaji said to the man, "rolling and moving in a crib?" He let a moment pass and then added, "That child is practicing yoga!"

The man nodded, and then Jnananandaji said to him, "Come up and show us." The man, to his credit, came up and did what Mahatmaji had asked.

Later Dhirananda was laughing, and Jnananandaji replied, "When you come to me you will get a different answer than from the other Swamis!" Sri Jnanananda truly is an original.

****

In 1962, China was threatening India, and they gave India three days to respond. Political leaders came to Anandamayi Ma[16] to find out what to do.

On the first day, many were gathered, all wanting answers.

---

[15] Self Realization Fellowship—an organization started by the Indian saint Paramhansa Yogananda to spread the teaching of Kriya Yoga. It is headquartered in Los Angeles, California, in the United States.

[16] One of the great woman saints of India; mentioned in Yogananda's book *Autobiography of a Yogi*.

"What day is today?" Ma said.

"Monday," came a hesitant reply.

"And tomorrow?" asked Ma.

"Tuesday," someone whispered.

"And the next day?" Ma asked, but nobody would reply and neither would Ma.

The next day when they came, she was in a different bhav,[17] and she pointed at the Himalayas and said, "Look, the clouds have cleared away from the mountains."

The next day, in the paper, China had announced it was not going to attack.

****

Ma had told Jnananandaji that anyone who had her darshan would be protected when they most needed it.

One man got his horoscope done, and they said he would die on a certain day in a car crash, but he just mentally dismissed it. Then, one day he was in a crash, and the crash was quite severe, but somehow he escaped unhurt.

Later, he took his chart to another astrologer without revealing that it belonged to him.

"Why have you brought me the chart of a dead man?" the astrologer asked.

---

[17] A bhav is a spiritual attitude or feeling. Ma was famous for having different spiritual bhavs.

The man then admitted that the chart was his own.

"Do you have a Guru?" the astrologer asked.

"Yes," the man replied, "Anandamayi Ma is my Guru."

The astrologer smiled and replied, "Where Anandamayi Ma begins, astrology ends."

****

The young Jnanananda often went to visit Anandamayi Ma, although He never went to ask questions—he went for her darshan. The whole time the Mahatma knew her, He only asked one question:

"Ma," Mahatmaji asked one day, "I feel like you know me better than I know myself, and I am confused how this is possible."

Ma's reply:

"There is only the One. There is no other."

****

I chanted "Hey Bhagavan" at a satsang with Sri Jnanananda. "I thought it would be good," Mahatmaji said, "but that was much better than I expected."

He then said with a smile, "While you were singing, I heard a woman's voice. We are surrounded by invisible beings."

Strangely, I had always felt like perhaps some angel helps me with music, and I feel this may have been a little hint to the identity of my helper.

He also said that Anandamayi Ma used to sing this chant beautifully.

****

Mahatma used to say that there are four chapters to the book of your life: the waking state, the dreaming state, the deep sleep state, and the state of the soul. The state of the soul is referred to in India as "turiya." By studying the first three states, one might perceive the state of turiya.

Most people are completely unaware of the soul.

Anandamayi Ma used to come to Mahatmaji more in dreams than in the waking state.

Once, Asangananda (a name given to Jnanananda by Ma) dreamed that Ma was on one hill, and that He was on another. She was holding a snake and whirling it around over her head (here Mahatmaji made a motion over His head like one would do with a lasso).

At one point in the dream, Ma released the snake and it flew towards Asangananda, but then He caught it and began whirling it around His head as well. Then He woke up.

Anandamayi Ma

****

Sri Jnananandaji sometimes gives homework. He once gave the homework to a Colombian woman and her daughter to figure out where the heart symbol came from.

Later, they sent Him a greeting card covered in hearts where the two ends at the bottom did not quite touch. When you turned the card sideways, you could easily see the Om symbol.

The card was for Guru Purnima, but did not mention anywhere inside that they had come upon the answer. It was a strangely perfect gift that brought the Mahatma much joy. It was a source of conversation at satsang for days.

****

Jnananandaji gave me His poem "The Individual" and asked me to read it aloud for everyone. "It contains my whole philosophy of life," the Mahatma said.

Later, He told me it was all right to give it to others. "No copyright," He said, "only all right!" And He laughed.

Jnanananda's laugh reminds me of the line from *Autobiography of a Yogi* describing Yogananda's Guru Sri Yukteswar, "When his laugh rang jovially, children looked upon him as their own."

****

Dharma[18] and I are much closer now—I even got to feed him. Then he rubbed his face all over me to let me know we are really friends.

One of Jnanananda's disciples had a dream about Dharma and how Dharma had become a dog. In this dream, every event and bit of karma that led to Dharma's incarnation as a dog was carefully revealed. As the dream was drawing to a close, Dharma started barking into the man's lower back and in the dream the man's kundalini was awakened.

The shock of the awakening kundalini was such that it woke the man from sleep, where he found that the kundalini was still awake. Tears of gratitude and joy streamed down the man's face, and in that great awakening, the man forgot the details that had been so carefully outlined in his dream about the karma of Dharma, the dog who was not a dog.

---

[18] Dharma is the dog that was the "police" of the ashram. Actually, the Maharaj said that he was not a dog—a point covered later in the book. This little policeman took his job very seriously; he had bitten over 300 people in his years of service! So, his affection, here described, was not so easily won!

Dharma and Maharaj

****

Once, a young man from Ananda was visiting Jnanananda, but Dharma seemed quite upset and was barking and barking, and the young man thought it would never end. Then, suddenly, the young man was seized with an inspiration and bowed with respect before Dharma. Then the barking stopped.

"You see," said Mahatmaji, "what you have done was, indeed, correct."

****

Quality, and not quantity, is what counts in kriya. Kriya is self offering, and kriya is purification.

****

Attitude and intention are everything, even in outward rituals. Mahatmaji related to me this story about two men talking about rituals:

Once, a man asked about making offerings to the deceased.

27

"If you do not believe," the other man replied, "then nothing will happen."

"If you do believe, then what is offered, you yourself will receive when you pass on."

****

Maitreyi[19] said that there are male stones, female stones, and eunuch stones. Most of the stones for her house are young and feminine. She said she can hear them sing, but that they do not sound like humans singing.

****

Once, a saint came to visit Jnananandaji at Maitreyi's house. He took only one step in and then stopped and said, "This whole house is singing."

****

Once, Jnanananda said that mantra CDs are not worth listening to.

"The mantra has to come from inside," Mahatmaji said, "otherwise maybe only the CD will find enlightenment."

Someone later asked Mahatmaji about how to read, and He replied, "Read a book until the book reads you."

---

[19] Maitreyi is the owner of what Jnananandaji called His "campsite," which was a house in Dehradun in Northern India. By the time I met him, Maharaj had stopped His wanderings and stayed in Maitreyi's house. She is also a wonderful soul.

"A mantra is the same," Mahatmaji added, "it must be repeated until you can hear it resounding all around you. Then you can stop chanting the mantra, because you will hear it and see it all around."

✳✳✳✳✳✳✳✳✳✳✳✳✳✳✳✳

Tonight I killed the kirtan with Jnananandaji. It was, indeed, the worst musical moment of this lifetime.

Jnananandaji's kirtan is all about joy, and each song a perfect reflection of that moment of joy as it passes through time.

Over the years, I have played the song Yogananda translated, "Receive Me on Thy Lap, O Mother," which is a very solemn and inward chant about the longing of the soul for the Divine. So many people have told me how much they loved this chant, I thought I would share it with the group at Mahatmaji's satsang.

What I forgot, was that it came from a thought that others had liked this song, and not from true inspiration. It also fell outside of the energy of the kirtan, and, as such, was a wonderful lesson in humility.

Right after the disaster, Dharma came and rolled around in my lap and let me pet his tummy. It was so sweet. I think he did not want me to feel too bad about the mishap.

Later, Dharma came and licked me, and Jnanananda had been talking about my name and that it means "crown" or "wreath."

"Maybe one day," Mahatmaji said, "you will be the crown of Ananda."

Thinking in terms of Ananda Sangha,[20] I thought, "Not likely." And He answered my thought by saying, "Ananda Brahma."[21]

"True joy," the Mahatma reminded me, "comes from the connection with God as ever new joy."

****

When I first met the Mahatma, He was living in the house of Maitreyi, a devotee with a house in Dehradun. Still, He often told stories about His days in Mussoorie, and so one day I decided to take a pilgrimage to see the holy place where Mahatmaji's leela had partially played out.

Inside was an unforgettable photo of Atmananda (Jnananandaji's Guru) and Rajarsi (Yogananda's most advanced disciple) together in America. Atmanandaji had gone to receive the sanyas mantra for Jnananandaji.

In that little kutir (probably at most 10 feet by eight feet of space) was a whole world.

Mahatmaji said He used to have 23 people stuffed into that space for a kirtan! Guests ranged from military generals to the pop singer Sting, who played cymbals while the Mahatma chanted.

---

[20] Ananda Sangha is an organization I was working with at the time that works with kriya yoga.

[21] Ananda Brahma means the bliss of the Self or the bliss of the creator.

The devotee who owned that land had passed on, and his son is a drinker who did not share his father's spiritual enthusiasm. Later, bills were not paid and the house fell into ruin. The chowkidar[22] took ownership, and, later, even the mafia was involved.

Everything is subject to change.

Maharaj with a small kutir he designed for sadhu life in Dehradun

---

[22] A chowkidar is a hired caretaker.

Maharaj outside the kurit in Mussoorie

****

Atmananandaji told Jnananandaji that there are sending and receiving stations in the body, but that most people's are in a broken condition.

"Oh yes," Mahatmaji added with enthusiasm, "even small insects like ants and bees can communicate over great distances. I once heard an ant say to another, 'Come over here and eat some of this ladu!'"[23]

****

"The Bermuda Triangle," Jnanananda once said, "You must have heard of it?" Thus began a story about the U.S. government, pyramids and yantras unlike I had ever heard before.

A devotee of Swamiji's was staying with two scientists who had researched the Bermuda Triangle. The U.S.

---

[23] Ladu is an Indian sweet.

government had found a city there deep under the ocean, and the city was in ruins, except for one pyramid. Inside of that pyramid was a sphere with a three dimensional Sri Yantra inside of it. The material was something like crystal, but not exactly; in fact, it is not actually known what substance it was made of.

After this, the devotee became fascinated with three dimensional Sri Yantras, and finally succeeded in making one out of wire. Later, this man's maid, not knowing what it was, threw it out, and thus ended that chapter of the devotee's life.

Sri Jnanananda said that the U.S. government had removed the crystal Sri Yantra from the pyramid, to take it to America for research, and once it was removed, the accidents in the Bermuda Triangle stopped.

"The Yantra," Mahatmaji added, "had 43 triangles, one for each letter of the Sanskrit alphabet. Sanskrit is not a man-made language—it came from inside."

"As you increase your vibration through kriya yoga, you will see this. Each chakra has petals, and each petal has a sound, as well as a taste, a feeling, a smell, and a color."

****

Sri Jnanananda told us that when He first started making yantras, fifteen minutes into it He was told that the forest where He lived was burning down. Everywhere the fire raged, but it did not touch His kutir or the house nearby. "That," Mahatmaji added, "was the only part of the forest left unburned."

After that, Mahatmaji decided to only make yantras on Durga Puja.

People say that there are two festivals per year for Divine Mother, one of which is Durga Puja, but really there are four. There are two secret ones, and that makes one every three months.

Mahatmaji made His first yantra using a compass, then He traced it, and He used the tracing to make further ones.

****

Swamiji answers every question you have, even the unspoken ones, or ones that you did not even know you had.

Maitreyi was commenting one day, saying that computer screens used to be dangerous. Jnanananda said, "Going to another ashram is dangerous!" (I had been planning on going to see one the very next day!)

Then He added, "Email is dangerous. Websites are dangerous." Interesting that the Mahatma, of all the things that He could have commented about, chose email and websites, which. at the time, was how I was earning my living.

****

"To have a house as a householder is good fortune, but to have one as a Swami is disastrous. Brahmacharis can have houses though," He added with a smile.

****

"Children can see things adults can't, but usually by the time they can talk, that ability is gone."

"It is because they have been trained to look at things. We look at objects, but what is between them?"

Then Mahatma said, "Like here." And He pointed into space. I tried to look in between and see what Mahatmaji could see, and for a moment I almost could.

"Suffer the little children to come unto Me," Christ said, "for such is the kingdom of Heaven."

****

Sri Jnanananda Maharaj had some fascinating thoughts about the leela of Radha and Krishna. One day in satsang He said:

"Radha is the individualized soul, and Krishna the universal soul. There are thousands of Radhas, or individualized souls, seeking union with the Infinite.

Krishna dances with each gopi,[24] and each gopi is so involved that they can only see that moment. There are said to be 16,000 gopis, but the truth is that there are many more—male and female both. When you add the devotion of all those gopis together, then you have Radha."

****

---

[24] Gopi literally means "a female cowherd" or "milkmaid," but in the context of Krishna, it usually means "lovers of Kirshna" or "lovers of the Divine."

Jnanananda was reading commentary by Lahiri Mahashaya about the *Bhagavad Gita*,[25] chapter 7, verse 3. The commentary said:

Out of a thousand, one seeks me, and of a thousand that seek, the one who finds me is a kriya yogi!

****

Lahiriji disliked organizations and wanted kriya to spread naturally, like the fragrance of a flower.

"Look at the birds," Jnanananda commented one day, "Eventually they push their young out of the nest and let them fly. Organizations are okay," Mahatmaji commented, "but eventually you have to learn to fly on your own."

****

At a satsang, Jnanananda asked me to read a passage from His book to my friend Daniel who was visiting from America. The very next day, He handed me the copy He had of *Transcendent Journey*.[26]

This was one of the most intense moments that I have ever had with Jnanananda. He asked me never to give the book away. Others can read it, but never give it away. "Hold it as a gift," He said, "and hold it close to your heart."

The copy He gave me was the last one that He had (though He was holding one more that He had promised to someone already), and it would be some time before another printing. The book came with

---

[25] The *Bhagavad Gita* is an excerpt from the *Mahabharata*, which is the epic tale of Krisha and Arjuna on the battlefield of life.

[26] *Transcendent Journey* is Mahatmaji's own autobiography.

tremendous power and blessing. I felt a wave of blessing rush over me as He gave me the book, and I tried to receive as much of it as I could.

Later, Jnananandaji said, "I like the way you read." He made a joke about how one of His own devotees had a misunderstanding about information in the book. Then He said that would not happen to me.

"Read this book once for the meaning, overall, and then dive deep into each sentence, and read the book until it reads you."

****

Dancing is a divine art form, and Jnanananda said you could dance your way to God. That kind of dancing is not the kind you do on stage in front of others, but alone with God. Dancing for God, Jnanananda said, is extremely good for health.

Shiva as Nataraj dances everything into creation. At the beginning of the kirtan that night, Jnanananda played Ananta Hari Om. "That," He said, "is the beginning," the first slow and deliberate movements of Shiva's cosmic dance.

****

"Everyone is born original, but most people die as copies." Jnananandaji loved to quote this sentence, which He claimed that He had once read in a newspaper. Mahatmaji added, "If you are original, there is no need for competition. All you have to do is be yourself."

At this time, my friend Daniel, who is a professional comedian and performer, was visiting, and I strongly felt Jnanananda had added this for his sake.

****

Superficial people tell Jnananandaji to learn more chants. "They want entertainment," the Mahatma commented one day, with a smile. And yet each of Asangananda's chants is ever new, and always fresh, each one reflecting the perfection of that particular divine moment. On Radhastami,[27] two weeks after Janamashtami,[28] Jnananandaji enlightened us further on this topic.

"All I have to do is think of Radha," Mahatmaji said, "and the chant will reflect that. If you talk to someone in London, you are in London. If you think about Brindavan, then you are in Brindavan."

****

There was a young French man who came to Atmanandaji in Kolkata. At a kirtan, he went to take a bath in Ma Ganga, and came back with a Shiva lingam that he had materialized! Atmanandaji asked where he had learned to do this, and the man said that he had learned from a Tibetan yogi in Paris. The man had other powers too, some of which he demonstrated, but Jnananandaji said He heard this second hand and did not actually witness those events. Jnananandaji had a tendency to stay within the walls of the ashram, and would not usually venture into town, or out at all, except with His Guru.

---

[27] Radhastami is the celebration of the birth of Sri Radha, consort of Sri Krishna.

[28] Janamashtami is the celebration of the birth of Sri Krishna.

Later, the man went to South India, and while he was there, another yogi took his spiritual powers!

✶✶✶✶✶✶✶✶✶✶✶✶✶✶✶✶

Jnananandaji asked His Guru about how to protect yourself, and the Guru answered, "Guru mantra."

Jnananandaji then added, "The Guru mantra is a shield. It gives you tremendous protection."

✶✶✶✶✶✶✶✶✶✶✶✶✶✶✶✶

The *Book of Mirdad* is a book about the man who was the Guru of Noah. Jnananandaji must have mentioned this book at least six times in two days, and even gave a suggestion about where to acquire the book in India. He also mentioned the strange and interesting fact that Noah comes from the word "nao," which means boat.

My friend Daniel, who is Jewish, was there at that time. I had the strong feeling the repeated suggestions were for his benefit.

✶✶✶✶✶✶✶✶✶✶✶✶✶✶✶✶

Jnananandaji once met the man who wrote *The Book of Mirdad*. The author himself gave a copy of the book to Asangananda. When talking about the book, Jnananandaji quoted the following passage:

> He who forgets this world is a devotee.
> He who forgets heaven is a saint.
> He who forgets the ego is liberated.
> He who forgets all he forgot is Self Realized.

✶✶✶✶✶✶✶✶✶✶✶✶✶✶✶✶

Jnanananda spoke also about a book by a man named Ram Alexander entitled *Death Must Die*, about a disciple of Anandamayi Ma. (Ram Alexander lives near Ananda in Assisi, Italy.) The book is about a sanyasi named Atmanananda, who took sanyas from Ma's Mother. Asangananda said, "Ma never took sanyas. She was beyond all that."

****

Tonight when I called to ask Jnananandaji if I could come to the satsang He said, "Are you coming with anyone?"

"No Sir, I am coming alone," I answered.

"Then the whole Universe is coming," He replied.

****

I told Jnananadaji that, right now, Swami Kriyananda[29] was in Goa.

"Right now, all roads lead to Goa," He replied.

Jnananandaji then told me a story about Goa. Once, Mahatmaji had gone with two other sanyasis to meet a woman from Goa whose husband had died. For years, she had been depressed, without even a smile, and so friends had asked the Swamis to talk with her, and they brought Sri Jnanananda along.

One of the Swamis was from Ramakrishna Mission, and the other from a different organization, and

---

[29] Swami Kiryananda is a kriya yogi initiated by Yogananda. I had the great good fortune to spend some time with Kriyanandaji in his ashram in India during that time.

young Jnananandaji was there as well. Since Mahatmaji was young, He let the other swamis do most of the talking, but all the time He was praying to His Guru, "You must have sent me here for a reason, so why have you sent me?"

To everything that the Swamis would say the woman would reply, "Yes, I have heard this all before." Then, as the Swamis were about to leave, Jnanananda asked if He could stay with her alone for a moment.

"Do you ever think about your husband?" Mahatmaji asked.

"I feel that is all I ever think about," she replied.

"Do you ever feel your husband in your heart?" He asked.

"I feel him so much in my heart sometimes I feel that he is all that is there," she replied.

"Then how is it that he is gone?" Jnananandaji asked.

The words struck home. She called a few hours later and said to Mahatmaji, "I am feeling a little happy."

****

I listened to a CD where Jnananandaji sings like Sri Pad Baba. We listened together. I felt He wanted me to actively call Sri Pad Baba, and He set up a vibrational resonance with me by listening to the music together. But it was more than listening—it was like a doorway, although I am not sure I was capable enough to totally walk through it.

"Sri Pad Baba," Mahatmaji said, "always wrote and sang origin-al songs." (Sri Jnanananda had a wonderful way of accenting the word origin when He would say "original.") "What is origin-al," He had said before, "is that which comes from your own origin."

Sripad Baba

****

At the end of a satsang, outside the gate on the street, Swamiji related to me this interesting story:

"When I was a young man, I asked my Guru if one day I would have disciples of my own. My Guru paused and smiled his big Bengali smile and then said 'Yes, but they will all be Gurus.'"

Then, with a twinkle in His eye, Jnananandaji added, "I am still meditating on what that means."

****

Once I had to leave India for Italy because India had changed the laws about tourist visas. I mentioned this to Asangananda and that we would have to leave for two months every six months if we did not get another kind of visa.

Then Mahatmaji asked, "Why?"

"Terrorism," I replied.

"Yes," He said, "but this, too, is a kind of terrorism!"

****

Jnananandaji has a way of making everyone feel like the intense state of joy that He is always in is within their reach. Tonight I was playing with Dharma, and everyone was watching, and Jnanananda said, "Dharma wants to play with Brahmachariji."

I could feel that the respect of the "ji" in the title came from His feeling the potential of God in me, and it reminded me of when Yogananda asked Swami Kriyananda about playing Christ in a crèche[30] scene.

"I would rather be a Christ than look like one," Swami Kriyananda said.

Yogananda replied, "That will come."

****

---

[30] A crèche is a live reenactment of the birth of Christ; also known as a nativity scene.

When Jnanananda was talking about us going to Italy He asked if I had read about Saint Francis. He said I would "get into it when I was in Assisi." And He also said that Francis was a great renunciate who kept nothing.

We were going to Assisi ostensibly because of visa issues, but Mahatmaji could see more, and He looked at me deeply and said, "Everything happens for a reason... everything!"

****

An older man and woman were married, but they did not want children or that kind of thing, so they went to Chidanandaji[31] and asked him for his blessing for them to go into the Vanaprastha ashram, which is usually not taken until after 50 years or so of age.

Mahatmaji said that first comes brahmacharya, and then grihastha, or the householder stage, and then vanaprastha, or the retirement stage, and by 75 years or so of age all people should be sanyasis.

"It was also this way in rural Switzerland," Mahatmaji said.

Generally, Swiss people built a small house above the level of the farmhouse to retire in. They called it the "first floor" even though it was not built on the ground level—the reason being that because it was intended for Divine use, it was not thought of as touching the ground!

---

[31] Chidanandaji was a great saint and devotee of Swami Shivanandaji of Rishikesh. He later headed up The Divine Life Society.

Later, the Swiss and other cultures lost this rich tradition, but Jnananandaji said they would eventually find it again.

Interestingly, the rural Swiss also had a tradition of the Divine Hour: a time in the afternoon, at twilight, when there was no work and people would just relax or meditate.

Swiss farmers used to pile cow manure outside their houses and make them into beautiful braids. This was a sign of good fortune.

Swami Chidanandaji

****

Jnanananda had a devotee who was a captain in the Navy. He was a great devotee of Varuna, who is the devata[32] of the sea.

In joyful service, the devotee bundled up a copy of *Transcendent Journey* and Jnanananda's poem "The

---

[32] Devata is often translated as "God," but, for most Westerners, a more accurate translation would be "angel," because it is not referring to the Absolute, but to an aspect of the divinity responsible for a certain part of creation.

Individual" together and dropped them into the bottom of the ocean.

Jnananandaji laughed and then said, "Varuna won't visit with him anymore because he is too busy reading!"

****

One of Jnananandaji's disciples worked in the World Trade Center. The night before the 9/11 attacks, he felt to take his computer home, although that was not his usual practice. Then, the morning of the event, he had a profound meditation and felt to meditate longer than usual.

Later, he got a call not to come to the office because there was no longer any office to come to. There was an Israeli man and a Chinese man working in the same office as this man, but they had not arrived to the office late.

****

Rajesh Sharma, the fellow working in the World Trade Center, had a back problem. He came to visit Jnananandaji, and the Mahatma asked Rajesh to meditate in a certain way under a tree.

It is an African tradition to teach this communion with nature to specific children identified by certain facial characteristics. (The facial characteristics are ways of identifying those initiated in previous lives.) They assure the validity of the initiate by placing the child underwater to see if he can swim. (Jnanananda assured me that they rescue the ones that cannot swim!)

The meditation happens by placing your back on the trunk of a tree with your left palm facing and touching the tree. The right hand goes over the heart, and then you feel the energy of the tree.

For Rajesh, thirty minutes was enough to cure his chronic back pain.

I should add that Jnanananda asked me to practice this technique twice when I came to see him, although I had never told Him that I had back pain during the exact time He recommended that I practice.

****

In 2011, some people from Ananda visited Jnanananda and asked Him about 2012. He said that was the first that He had heard of it.

Then they asked what would happen, and He said they would all become jivanmuktas.[33]

"There are two kinds of jivanmuktas," the Mahatma added, "those who know that they are free, and those who do not know."

****

When Jnanananda was a young man, He learned a profession: He became a chocolatier.

He said it was possible to have out-of-body experiences where your body continues to do what it needs to do.

---

[33] A jivanmukta is a Self-realized soul.

Once, while making chocolates, He took a journey and came back to find himself in His body making chocolates.

A man He knew in Bengal used to leave the body while driving, eventually to find himself safely back home.

****

A Swamini came to visit Asangananda with two young Brahmacharis to see what Mahatmaji, this foreign Swami, was all about. She was not quite sure if He was really up to the high level of a "real" sanyasi.

Her first question: "How many meals do you eat in a day?"

"You see," Jnanananda paused the story to clarify, "there is a hierarchy amongst sanyasis. If you eat only once a day, that is good. If you eat twice, that perhaps is okay, but three times, well... not so good."

So with great enthusiasm Jnananandaji answered, "Once."

Then one of the Brahmacharis asked the Swamini for permission to speak, which was then granted, and he asked, "At what time do you take that meal?"

Swamiji answered, "From morning until night."

Years later, the Swamini returned, but this time with a different attitude.

****

A man used to pass in front of Jnananandaji's house and, after years, one day they began to chat.

The man had some problems with his legs, and Jnananandaji said, "Why not talk to your legs and give them gratitude for carrying you so many places for so many years? You can keep taking medicine if you like, but why not talk to your legs?"

Within a few months, the man was 80% better, and, a little while later, he recovered completely.

Years later, the man approached Mahatmaji and mentioned that his wife was losing her sight. She had a cataract in one eye and a detached retina in the other. They went to Bangalore for an operation, which failed. Later, she got better, to which Jnananandaji told the man, "It is because of you. You must have told her to practice this gratitude."

Of course the man suspected that Jnananandaji's grace may have had something to do with it, but it was also a lesson in gratitude.

✳✳✳✳✳✳✳✳✳✳✳✳✳✳✳✳✳

"Everyone is born original, but most people die as copies." Mahatmaji was quite fond of this quote, which He had once read in a newspaper. "Even on the spiritual path," He said one day, "most of them are copies."

"The whole aim of modern education," He said, "is to create good copies." Then He added, "You must be careful for that."

"When you come from your origin, there is no need to compete. Also, there is no need to chase after money.

Money, at that point," Mahatmaji added with a smile, "will be chasing after you!"

✶✶✶✶✶✶✶✶✶✶✶✶✶✶✶✶

After asking a certain question, Jnananandaji related the story of the young man who manifested a Shiva lingam in the Kolkata ashram, only to return later, his powers taken away by a yogi from South India. "Any powers that can be given," He said, "can also be taken away."

"Take yourself light-ly," Mahatmaji used to say. "Not seriously—even as a being of light."

✶✶✶✶✶✶✶✶✶✶✶✶✶✶✶✶

Sri Jnanananda knew two scientists. One had discovered a way to make energy from air, and it was enough energy to propel something to the moon and back again. This technology was purchased by the government and then hidden.

One of the scientists himself was in hiding, although he did not mention this to Maharaj.

Eventually, that man went to South India to a cave to practice yoga. Jnananandaji himself had seen the cave.

Later Jnananandaji received a letter from this man: "Have failed in attempt at yoga, will return to science."

Another scientist Jnananandaji knew had created something about the size of a small book that could create enough energy to run several households. This man was also in hiding.

****

With a group of foreigners, mostly from America, Jnananandaji said, "It states clearly in the Bible that humans are not to eat the fruit of the tree of knowledge."

"The fruit of the tree of knowledge is money. Knowledge should not be traded for money or commercialized. This is clearly written in the Bible."

****

Talking again about the Bible, Jnananandaji said that man was born into paradise. The plants, the birds, and animals all lived in harmony. Animals did not kill or eat each other—they learned this later from mankind.

"To take the life of anything," Mahatmaji said, "is murder. Of course we take life by accident, while walking we step on something, but to consciously take any life is murder."

In the Bible it says that God created man from clay (which means the earth) and breathed His life into it.

"The same breath that is moving in you, is moving in me. The air that comes from your breath is, a moment later, in me, and then in Dharma, and so on.

Consciously taking that breath from anything is murder—nothing less."

****

Sri Jnanananda asked me what was my favorite part of the satsang the night before. I thought for a moment and then said "Gee Sir, I do not know."

"It is because his favorite part is every part."

Everyone laughed because they could feel that He had, as always, spoken the Truth.

****

Mukunda, a very special child, and friend of the Mahatma, came one day to his parents asking for a bandage and some medicine on his wrist. Looking carefully, his parents protested that nothing at all was wrong with his wrist.

"There is nothing wrong there now," the little one replied, "but there will be tomorrow."

The parents complied and bandaged the wrist.

The next day, they carefully inspected the wrist, but there was nothing there.

In the eyes of Mukunda, it was not there because it had already been cared for.

"You see," Jnananandaji said, "prevention is the best cure."

****

Jagjivan Bapu was a saint and also a friend of the Mahatma. Some of the adults at Jagjivan Bapu's would sneak away from the ashram to smoke. (Smoking was strictly forbidden in Bapu's presence.)

One day, Jnanananda was out to walk in the woods and came upon Mukunda in a clearing, but the boy did not see him. The young boy held in his hand the dry part of a piece of grass, and was bringing it to his lips and then away and exhaling, just like the piece of grass was a cigarette.

When Mukunda saw Mahatmaji, he quickly pretended he was using the dry grass to clean his feet. The young boy, only three years old at that time, was very clever.

"You see," said Mahatmaji, "Children are great imitators."

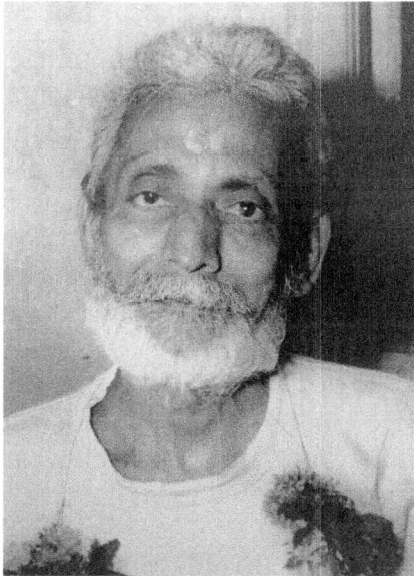

Jagjivan Bapu

Maharaj with Jagjivan Bapu

****

When Jnananandaji was a young man, He disobeyed
His Guru and went for darshan at Jagganath Puri.
When He got there, they would not let Him in because
He was a foreigner. Someone took pity on the young
man, though, and brought Him some prasad.

As it turns out, that prasad was unclean, and as a
result of eating it Jnananandaji caught jaundice. He
entrained at once for Kolkata.

"By the time He got to the ashram," his gurubhai
Paramanananda said, "He was as yellow as a
mountain of butter!"

The young Swiss man ate only katcha (unripe) papaya
(cooked of course) and milk for ten days and was
cured.

This story came with a big smile, and, at the end, with
an air of comical pride, Mahatmaji added, "The cure
was from my own observations—not from my Guru."

****

"I will tell you something," Jnanananda said, and then quickly added, "Babaji can only be seen from the inside."

"He is both a male and a female.

He is both man and God.

I have not written this in the book... no, certain things I have left out. But it is true, Babaji can be seen only from the inside."

****

There was a rabbi who used to teach by telling stories. One story he told was of a very wise king and his assistant.

The assistant came to the king and told him that this year, because of the food, everyone would become mad. (And here Mahatmaji made a face to indicate that He meant crazy.)

The king was very concerned, and, at this time, kings very much loved their subjects—and so the two men thought.

After a moment, the assistant said, "Sir, there is enough food from last year to feed you and your family, and me and my family."

The king thought for a moment and said, "You have not given me good advice. If all the people go mad, and you and I are sane, everyone will think that we are mad and they will throw us out!"

"You see," Mahatmaji added, "you can't govern unless you are equally mad. Political scientists—they are also a little bit mad. When you are unfit for anything else, you become a politician."

Interestingly, this story came just after a devotee was telling a not-very spiritual story, in a not-very spiritual way. At the time, I was wondering how Jnanananda dealt with not always being in a high spiritual environment. This story was the immediate answer to my question.

Sri Jnanananda would answer every question that I had, even the ones that only entered into my mind, at times ones even unnoticed by me.

One time, long ago, I had this thought in the back of my mind, wondering if the traditional wooden shoes that yogis wear would ever develop imprints of where the feet were, or if they were too hard for that.

One day, Maharaj was talking about a pair of wooden sandals that He had given to someone and He said, "They were worn where the feet were," and then He flashed me one of His amazing smiles.

In that smile was everything.

****

"Nobody knows where he will go and when he will go," the Maharaj said about me one night as I was taking His leave.

With a smile, He added, "No appointments, no disappointments!"

When I arrived for satsang, Swamiji sat me down, and He lit the incense in His usual way. As He began talking, I could see that the smoke from the incense was mirroring His thoughts and words.

At one moment after He finished a thought, a whole section of smoke rolled itself quickly into a ball like a period.

During that moment, He was talking about originality.

"When it comes to songs," Mahatmaji said, "I am a great thief. I have taken songs even from a beggar." (Later, in a different satsang, He told me that this was on the train from Haradwar[34] to Dehradun, and that the song was His version of "Sri Ram, Jai Ram," and that the beggar had sung the song using two rocks to keep the time.)

"Yet I am not good at copying the songs of others," Mahatmaji said.

Swamiji's songs always in some way reflect the moment, just as the smoke was reflecting the Mahatma's words.

"The most important book to read," Sri Jnanananda went on, "is the book of your life. The book of your life has four chapters: your waking life, your dreaming life, your life in the state beyond dreams, and the life of the soul, which is called 'turiya.'"

---

[34] Haridwar is a sacred city in Uttarakhand, India, at the foothills of the Himalayas. Haridwar would mean the abode of Vishnu or Krishna. Maharaj was of the opinion that the place belonged to Shiva, and thus always pronounced this town Haradwar.

"The most important thing when reading the book is not what takes place; the most important thing is your attitude." Mahatmaji then paused for a moment, and added with a subtle force, "Attitude is the most important thing."

Never one to repeat a point, I felt there was deep meaning in this, both personal and impersonal.

You see, everyone creates their own reality.

****

I had always had a slight aversion to the Indian tradition of people feeding one another with their hands, and then one day out of the blue Swamiji said, "The sharing of food was part of the leela of Krishna and Radha—oh yes!"

Then He told the following story:

Once, He was with Gurudial Malik, and there were maybe six people all sitting to take their food, and Malikji said that nobody could take their food until Jnanananda took His.

Feeling inspired, Jnananandaji then took some food and put it into Malikji's mouth, and there was great laughter.

Then, on a more serious note, He added, "You see, there is a moment for everything!"

****

"You have read in the book the story of Sri Pad Baba and the bedbugs?"[35] Swamiji asked.

"Yes," I replied with a smile, and we both laughed. Then He added something I could hardly wrap my mind around.

"Sri Pad Baba used to sometimes take the siddhis of other yogis," Mahatmaji said simply. "One such yogi could replicate rail tickets and that sort of thing."

"This is holding them back," Sri Pad would say, and he would take it.

Then Jnananandaji reminded me of the story of the young man who came to YSS[36] who had a Tibetan Guru in Paris who could materialize Shiva lingams from the river, but who later lost that power.

****

"Swami Kriyananda is going to make a movie," Maharaj said one day.

"Now maybe YSS will make one, too. They have to compete with one another!"[37]

****

Mahatmaji said that Satya Sai Baba once stopped at Vashista Gufa on pilgrimage. (I believe He said it was on the way to Badrinath).

---

[35] Sri Pad Baba once cleared a house infested with bedbugs by sleeping with his foot on the wall. The story is related in *Transcendent Journey*.

[36] Yogoda Satsanga Society, the sister organization of SRF in India, was started by Paramhansa Yogananda.

[37] Later, in fact, they did make a movie!

Sai Baba said, "I will give you two thousand rupees."

Purushotamanandaji said, "One thousand would be enough."

Baba then produced the money. Nirvedanandaji was there and said that the money looked quite old.

Then Jnanananda said, "Oh yes, many yogis have these powers, moving things from here to there."

✳✳✳✳✳✳✳✳✳✳✳✳✳✳✳✳

Once, I was there when Mahatmaji had a slight cold. He called it the "unwanted guest."

"They used to take two weeks to clear in Switzerland," He said, "but in India they take only one."

Always looking for the message behind the words, I wondered if that was from the spiritual effects of India.

Immediately Mahatmaji added, "This is because of the climate."

✳✳✳✳✳✳✳✳✳✳✳✳✳✳✳✳

"Everyone is born with sending and receiving technology within, but most people's equipment is in a broken condition."

"The more you rely on cell phone, camera, recorder, et cetera, the less you will be able to access this inner technology."

✳✳✳✳✳✳✳✳✳✳✳✳✳✳✳✳

"In old age, the best medicine is food."

Jnananandaji quoted this and then added that food can help prevent certain diseases.

"And that was before all of the poison they add to food now, and who knows, what they have at a roadside stand may not suit your constitution."

Strangely, the very day He said that, I had switched roadside stands. I usually ate a dosa down the street before satsang, but that night I had tried something different, and it did not end up agreeing with my stomach.

Could the Mahatma see that the food had not agreed? Did the strength of His suggestion influence my stomach? I have always wondered about this.

****

Commenting once on the daughter of some devotees, Jnananandaji said, "I knew her when she was just a small girl. She is all grown up now and lives in America. She is a dentist."

Jnananandaji always said that for the renunciate, the whole world is His family. This statement about the dentist above was said with the same pride as if Jnananandaji Himself had been her father. It was a perfect illustration that He, indeed, was the Father of all.

****

"I used to wonder why Paramhansa Yogananda passed away so young, with so many problems with his body. I know at least one of the answers—it was Vitamin M."

Later, Swamiji explained that Nirvedananda from Vashista Gufa had coined the term "Vitamin M" to refer to money. Sadhus are not even supposed to use the word for money. Sri Pad Baba used to refer to money as "papers."

"You see," Maharaj said, "When Yogananda came to America, he had these twelve lessons. But the people protested that these would never sell, and to some extent they were right. I have seen those lessons, and they are only for the serious aspirant. So, later, they made 180 lessons, which are still very nice."

✳✳✳✳✳✳✳✳✳✳✳✳✳✳✳✳

Talking about Vitamin M got Jnananandaji onto the topic of marriage, because, traditionally, men had to go into the world to make money.

In Switzerland, Jnananandaji had asked why women did not have the right to vote. He found out that only those that carry a sword (which meant to serve in the military) have the right to vote.

"Voting, you see," Mahatmaji said, "was considered a dirty kind of a thing. In any case, it was usually the women at home telling the man whom to vote for!

Traditionally, men were the protectors of women, mostly physically. Women, in turn, had the job of protecting the man's soul.

You see, men had to go out in the world and earn money, which is dangerous for the soul, and the woman was supposed to protect him.

Nowadays, of course, this has all gone haywire.

In the *Bhagavad Gita* it says that the state of mankind rests in the hands of the women. The man, it hardly makes any difference, but the woman upholds the whole society. When that goes, everything will fall apart."

Mahatmaji then said, "I would add one thing, that in addition to protecting the wife, the husband should protect every woman, and in addition to protecting the husband's soul, the wife should protect the soul of every man."

****

When Jnananandaji first met Maitreyi, she told Him that money is very pure. So He asked, "How is that?"

"Money is very pure," she said, "It can quickly tell you the character of a man!"

Swamiji said that He would add then that both money and women were pure. Both could quickly tell you the character of a man.

"How you treat women," Mahatmaji added, "Is how you treat the Mother of the Universe."

****

In the library of Yogoda Math, Swamiji had come across a book by an American author which put forth the idea that teeth are devils. "Look at the work they do," Mahatmaji added.

Later, because of His love of sweets as a youth, Jnananandaji had to have His teeth removed. Paramananda, who lives in Florida, paid for an entire new set.

At the time, the dentist was on Upper Circular Road in Kolkata, and you could see all the people as they were walking by.

The dentist was trying to pull the tooth, but could not, and so called upon the assistant. Yet even the two of them could not do it together. So they resorted to calling in a man off of the street to help!

Later, the dentist said he had never seen a tooth with roots that deep.

"That," Jnanananda said, "is because I am a sadhu."

"Other people have all kinds of problems with their false teeth, so they get new ones, or have them fixed, but I have never had a problem with mine."

Before removing the teeth, He asked His Guru about removing them, and His Guru said, "Old friends," but he was not against it.

Commenting then on the books at Yogoda Math, Mahatmaji said there were many fine books there, but you read them at your own risk! He laughed and laughed.

There was a book written by a man in the 1930's about Eastern Sadhus invading the Americas. I think it is called *Hinduism Invades America*. In that book, the author says he could understand every sadhu who came, except for Swami Ram Tirtha, who remains a mystery.

Later, people said that Tirtha drowned, but Swamiji does not believe this. All sadhus know not to swim in the river.

"He disappeared from the eyes of the world," Swamiji said with a twinkle in His eyes.

****

Curious about the rule about Sadhus not swimming, I asked Swamiji why.

"Because it is dangerous," He replied, and He shared the following story:

There was a man named Robert Svoboda who used to come to Mahatmaji's kutir in Mussoorie. He was a famous author of books about jyotish[38] and other things. He came with a boy of about 21 years of age, who was Robert's disciple. The boy's parents were wealthy and quite high up in the American military.

Robert came to Jnananandaji with a plan for the whole trip up into the Himalayas. This many days here, then to Uttarkashi this many days, and eventually they would come back to Dehradun where they were to do a havan[39] for the house.

"Why even go at all?" Sri Jnananandaji said, "When you have already gone in your own mind?"

Nevertheless, off they went.

---

[38] Jyotish is Vedic Astrology.
[39] Havan is a ritual fire ceremony.

There was a different man who Jnanananda knew, who had been in the Israeli military and, later, written a book about that experience. After his time in the military, he had become a sadhu and was in Uttarkashi at Shivananda Ashram, which is a little outside of the town.

This man had asked at the ashram where there was a safe place to take a bath, as it was rainy season and the river was in flood. They took him to a spot and the sadhu quickly replied, "I would NEVER take a bath there."

The very next day, Robert and the young man visited the same ashram, and were recommended to bathe in the same place that the sadhu had refused.

The boy entered first, but perhaps went a little too far, and his body turned around three times and then was gone.

There was no trace of the boy.

Later, the boy's parents came, and, with the help of the Indian army, they made a search for the boy.

They took a dummy and put it in the river at the very same place. They put it in the water, it spun around three times and then was gone, never to be seen again.

✱✱✱✱✱✱✱✱✱✱✱✱✱✱✱✱

"I have a special love for Indian sweets," Jnananandaji admitted one day with a sheepish grin. It was, after all, the very same day that the Maharaj had shared the story of losing His teeth.

"Even chocolate," He said with a smile. "People bring me chocolate from all over the world, but I prefer Cadbury Original. Of course, Cadbury is British," Mahatmaji commented, "but here they have Indianized it!"

Later on, I could not help but feel that this story was for me. At this time I was taking a little break from my own spiritual tradition, and traveling around India. Jnananandaji had remarked that it was best to go very deep into the original path that had been given to you by God.

Now, any chocolate lover—and especially one with the sensitivity of Sri Jnanananda—knows that Cadbury Original is simply not the best chocolate. The statement, then, was about loyalty.

To Sri Jnanananda, India had been the Guru, or at least the home of His own beloved Guru, and His home as well. "Loyalty," Paramhansa Yogananda had said, "is the first law of God." Here, Sri Jnananandaji was demonstrating that law quite beautifully.

****

A man once came to Jnananandaji and wanted to become a sadhu and, more specifically, a Swami. Jnananandaji said, "Okay," but first he would have to submit to a test.

Sri Jnanananda then asked if this man had even been to Bombay.

The man replied that he had not.

Then Jnananandaji asked if he had friends in Bombay.

Again he replied in the negative.

Jnananandaji said then that the man would have to go to Bombay on a train with no money or anything, and if he could make it back to Dehradun, then he had passed the test.

I was in awe, and Mahatmaji picked up the thought that was written so clearly on my face.

"You want to know how to do it?" He asked with a smile. Of course I nodded in assent.

"You get off at the train station in Bombay and you wait on the platform and observe the people to find someone who is local. You then approach the person and say, 'Excuse me, I am unfamiliar with Bombay and I would like to ask if you yourself know any beggars in Bombay?'"

"Naturally they would ask why," to which Mahatmaji would reply, "Because the most difficult thing is to look directly into the eyes of a beggar."

"By this time they are very curious," and then He added with a smile, "and they usually ask you to come for chai or something."

****

Long ago in Europe, it was common practice for young men just getting ready for their professional life to go wandering with no money for a few months.

They would stay by the rivers and get their food from the millers, who were in the business of grinding the wheat using the power of the river. Perhaps the young men would help a little, in exchange for a little food.

Then, with a slight shift in energy, Mahatmaji added, "By the time of my youth this practice was basically over—because of World War II."

****

When a group of mostly young American women came, Swamiji first received them in the garden, and then He invited them in the house, saying that all who enter this house are old.

"They were a little afraid to come in," Mahatmaji said. Then He clarified things for them by saying to them, "by that I mean ancient," and they understood that He meant the soul and not the body, and they were at ease again.

****

An insurance agent called once while we were waiting for satsang. In a voice of total sincerity, Mahatmaji said, "Yes, I have Ātma[40] insurance." Later, He commented that the lady on the line had seemed quite confused.

****

Jnanananda spoke about how Babaji could travel from mountain to mountain without walking. Even now, in America, there are people who have this power, but if they commercialize it even a little bit, then they will lose this power.

---

[40] Ātma means the "individualized soul."

"Sri Pad Baba had this power," Jnananandaji said. "I never saw him do it," the Mahatma said, "but I heard it from others."

****

The dentist lady from Los Angeles (mentioned in another story) got a copy of *Transcendent Journey* in the mail. The cover of *Transcendent Journey* has 17 stars on it, and she wrote a thank you letter on a card that just happened to have 17 silver stars on it as well—but only if you counted very carefully, because five of them were hidden in a tree on the card. When Mahatmaji handed me the card, He had to point out the hidden ones to me that brought the count up to 17.

God sends us countless messages in every moment, but how many of us are careful enough to see them?

****

This story once again brought into light the aspect of Jnananandaji as a Father. He was in the hospital when she was born (the dentist in the above story) "Even then," He said, "she was a very special person."

She was, in fact, the first young girl to play Radha in the Radha Krishna leela that Jnananandaji used to have the kids enact.

****

"What Paramhanda Yogananda gave was the blueprint of kriya yoga—the rest you have to fill in yourself. In the *Autobiography [of a Yogi]*, he says that kriya yoga will be your Guru, and one day this will be true for you, too."

"Did you read in the book that part about what the Girnar Mahatmaji asked me one night? There is an entire teaching there."

I was visiting on January 27, 2011, and it was the day after Republic Day. "I started that pilgrimage on Republic Day. You must remember that part about the Mahatmas meeting at midnight around the flame that has been burning since the time of Dattatreya?

I have heard that it has been destroyed. I am not sure—but I have heard. Perhaps torn down to build a hotel. This is the kind of thing that is happening everywhere."

****

As I was walking out one night, Jnananandaji Maharaj was asking if I had heard of the man in America who had wanted to sell his soul. He had offered this online.

"How much would he like for it?" I asked, and Mahatmaji laughed. Then as I was walking out, the realization hit me that nearly everyone in America is in some way selling their soul.

The Mahatma is always speaking on many levels. Just as I was writing this, it occurred to me that I had told Jnananandaji about an upcoming trip to America which was intended to make money, and realized that perhaps this story had also been a gentle warning.

****

There was a very learned man in M. Pradesh who became a Swami. He was head of the Chinmaya Mission, and in the 1950s he had written a book about the commercialization of the Guru. In the time of Lahiri Mahashaya, nobody (other than you and your Guru) knew who your Guru was. Even the Guru would not tell who were the disciples. He called it the Guru industry, and Jnanananda added, "You also can call it the yoga industry."

****

To be totally in tune with the Divine flow in every moment—that is Swami Jnanananda. So many lessons given on so many levels it is hard to know where to start. Here is a favorite from this trip:

When Jnanananda saw Dharma again rolling on my lap and playing with me, He said, "See, it is one year since Steve was here, and yet Dharma is playing with him."

There was a poignant pause and then Mahatmaji added with a smile, "You see, for Dharma and I there is no time!"

Maharaj

****

Once, Dharma was sick and needed very much a nebulizer, which is a device that helps you to inhale certain medicines. Jnananandaji stood there, nebulizer in hand, holding Dharma, and then looked straight at me and said, "You cannot love God and also love money."

****

When kriya is given in America, certain things are left out. That Om Namo Bhagavate Vasudevaya is the mantra of Badri Narayan, for example. These things, Jnanananda said, you must discover on your own by practice.

****

Jnanananda's view of renunciation is so pure. One day, He gently commented about a local teacher saying that "he made sadhus like a factory!" The comment was said with a joyful, and yet slightly disapproving, look.

Only one who gives everything is truly fit to inherit the kingdom of God.

✶✶✶✶✶✶✶✶✶✶✶✶✶✶✶✶✶

"Quality," Jnanananda said, referring to kriya, "is more important than quantity. I do not believe in those who do hundreds of kriyas. My Guru could have darshan of Shiva in one breath, and Shiva," Mahatmaji added with a smile, "is Badri Narayan."

✶✶✶✶✶✶✶✶✶✶✶✶✶✶✶✶✶

A special song for me, a hymn taught to me by Jnanananda which was introduced to Him by Paramanananda called "In the Garden." The chorus was changed by the Mahatma. The original was:

> And He talks with me and He walks with me and He tells me I am His Own.

Maharaj changed it to:

> And You walk with me and You talk with me and You tell me I am your own.

Jnanananda said, "In Christianity, they hold God away, they say that He talks to me, and not YOU talk to me." In India, often they use also the "tum" form of you, which is a more intimate form when speaking to God.

✶✶✶✶✶✶✶✶✶✶✶✶✶✶✶✶✶

After "In the Garden," He played the chant, "I am AUM." He had changed the lyrical structure and the words slightly. Every song, and every moment, were an expression of the Mahatma's origin-ality.

****

Jnananandaji got His first grey hair at 36. He was thrilled.

As a child He had prayed, "Make me old. Old people," He said, "are at the stage where they are the crown jewel of life—assuming they have lived rightly."

Once, this story was told to a group of yogis from America (he said it was an Ananda group), and they were quite shocked.

"Americans," He said, "have a tendency to worship youth."

****

I do not remember the exact words of the Mahatma surrounding this moment, but one night, while holding Dharma, He looked at me and said, "It is all restlessness."

****

There was a siddha yogi who had the power to reveal any aspect of Divine Mother to anyone. One of his disciples was a mahant[41] from Dehradun who begged for Her darshan. "Are you sure you can take it?" the yogi asked, but the mahant was convinced.

One night, at midnight, they went out to a secluded place where the yogi conjured up one of the most

---

[41] A Mahant is a Hindu priest or head of a temple or monastery.

fierce aspects of Divine Mother, and the mahant immediately passed out cold from fear.

There was much laughter in the room, but then Jnananandaji added, on a more serious note, that later that siddha yogi was in jail in Delhi. "Those siddha yogis," He said with a smile, "Always getting into trouble!"

****

When Jnananandaji was a young man, He was close with a man who was in His church. They were Reformists—not Lutheran, but like that.

One day, young Jnanananda showed up to the man with ten questions. "Can you answer my questions?" the boy asked innocently. This man was honest, and did not want to hurt the boy's faith, and I have a feeling the questions were quite above his head, even though from a young boy.

"No," the man answered honestly, "I do not have the answer to any of those questions."

****

A saint had given Jnanananda a book called *Nobody, Son of Nobody*. In this book, there are three kinds of people: Mr. Nobody, Mr. Somebody, and Mr. Everybody. Later, that book was taken from Him by a sadhu from Rishikesh.

I asked the Mahatma in jest, "Which one are you?" But I knew full well that Mr. Everybody will not reveal his true Presence, and Mahatmaji gently avoided the question.

Later, I was able to find a copy of the very same book and present it to the Mahatma as a gift.

****

Tonight, Jnananandaji told a whole series of stories to illustrate that God will provide for you.

Once, He was walking from Ranikhet to Kathgodam, and He was quite hungry. He came to a place where there were some food stalls for about 50 meters, near Neem Karoli Baba's ashram. He took to the center of the road and walked very slowly, not looking to the left, and not looking to the right. Slowly He walked through the stalls, but nobody called him, and He was just thinking, "I am cooked," when one called out, "Babaji, aiiye,"[42] and so He came. First, tea was offered, and then later, when they discovered His hunger ("I must have been staring at their food," He said with a smile), food was offered as well.

Another time, Mahatmaji was coming down from Mussoorie walking, this time with Maitreyi. Part way down she mentioned that she was hungry. Jnanananda saw some houses and approached one to ask a lady for water. Eventually, the man of the house came and offered them tea. Then neighbors came and a satsang started. Food was offered. Later, they inquired how He intended to get home, and He looked at their vehicle and replied, "By car," and everyone laughed heartily, and of course they gave them a ride home.

The Divine has infinite resources when handled by one who has offered everything and received everything in return.

---

[42] "Babaji, aiiye" translates to "Come, Father." It is similar to the way you might call a priest "Father."

****

Jnanananda saw something in the newspaper about the Nayaswami order and asked about the change of color.[43] I was sort of apologizing for it, saying that most of Swami Kriyananda's advanced disciples were married.

Jnanananda said, "That does not matter. The rishis themselves were married. What matters is self-control."

All these things are written in the scriptures. If you want to have a daughter or you want to have a son, everything is there, but people have forgotten.

****

Jnanananda showed me the rakhis[44] tied around the sacred trees outside Maitreyi's house. "You see," He said, "we all need the protection of nature—without that, we will perish."

****

Around Diwali there were less people than usual at the satsang. Maharaj's simple comment: "Around Diwali there are less people than usual—people are at

---

[43] Swami Kriyananda founded a new Swami order called the Nayaswami Order (naya means "new") and asked them to wear a blue color rather than the traditional ochre color worn by Swamis in India. One of the changes in that Order was that married and unmarried people were allowed to join the Order. Traditionally in India, only unmarried people can enter the Swami Order.

[44] A rakhi is a decorative string or bracelet given as a sign of protection.

home, with their families," and He added with a smile, "This is the right thing."

****

Saradananda was a man who spent most of his life in France. He came once to Swamiji with a few of his disciples, one of whom was an African man who was initiated into the common language of Africa. (There is a common language in Africa, but only for the initiated.)

This initiate taught Jnanananda tree therapy. All diseases, even those of other people, can be cured by tree therapy. You sit under a tree, with the left hand behind you on the tree and the right hand on the heart. You then center yourself and feel that you are one with the flow of energy in the tree.

****

"The cure of every disease is patience. That is why the sick one is called a patient. Patience is neutrality. Equanimity. In the face of this, all disease will cease."

Later Maharaj added, "The doctor must learn patience, too."

****

One day I was the first pilgrim to reach the campsite of Asangananda. I came quietly around the corner and was hit by a wall of silence. That silence was so complete, I could not even lift my hands to say namaste, and neither could I take a single step. In fact, no movement at all was possible in that wall of complete stillness.

Mahatmaji sensed my presence. Though I wished that moment could go on for Eternity, He slowly smiled and gave me His pranam. But the memory of that silence will stay with this pilgrim forever.

****

"I am full of stories," Mahatamaji said one day, "there is no end to my adventures!"

****

Asangananda taught himself how to talk in wooden sandals traditionally worn by sadhus. He walked from Mussoorie to Dehradun in these! Eventually, He had to give them up, and left them on the side of the road under a bush, because Sri Pad Baba was walking too fast.

Later, Sri Pad Baba got hold of some havai chappals[45] and wore one and gave the other to Jnananandaji. For a while they walked this way, each wearing one sandal, but later both chappals were given to Asangananda.

---

[45] Havai chappals are cheap plastic sandals.

Sripad Baba walking

****

When Shivani, Arjuna, and a group came to see Jnananandaji, they asked Him to come and visit Ananda. "I don't even go to Delhi," He laughed, but later He said to Arjuna, "If a sadhu goes somewhere, He only buys a one-way ticket."

Anandamayi Ma used to give this advice to disciples: do not make your spiritual journey a return-trip ticket.

There is deep meaning in this, actually.

✸✸✸✸✸✸✸✸✸✸✸✸✸✸✸✸

That night, Jnanananda asked me if I was going
forward to Pune or Gurgaon. "I don't know, Swamiji,"
I said, "I have not bought a return ticket."

✸✸✸✸✸✸✸✸✸✸✸✸✸✸✸✸

After my return ticket comment, Jnananandaji said to
me, "I have always thought of spiritual organizations
like colleges—there comes a time when it is right to
graduate."

✸✸✸✸✸✸✸✸✸✸✸✸✸✸✸✸

"Do you know what Sat means?" Jnanananda asked,
"Sat sangha."[46] He laughed. When Sat and sangha
are together, one of them has to go.

When sangha is there, then Sat has to go. Or if Sat is
there, then sangha will not be.

✸✸✸✸✸✸✸✸✸✸✸✸✸✸✸✸

In this same vein, Jnananandaji praised me for my
pilgrimage to Badrinath alone. His simple words: "A
real pilgrimage is done alone."

✸✸✸✸✸✸✸✸✸✸✸✸✸✸✸✸

"In 1980 I was in Pune—that was my last tour,"
Mahatmaji said with a little laugh. Sri Jnanananda
was staying at the time with one Mr. Malhottra, who
was a doctor for the Indian military and personally
responsible for the diet of all of the branches of the

---

[46] Sat means "Truth." Sangha means "community."

armed forces. Mr. Malhottra was a disciple of Om Baba and Sant Gulab Singh.

Once, Malhottraji was called away to Delhi, and, as he was leaving, Sant Gulab Singh mentioned to him that if anyone ever had chronic hiccup there was a simple and effective cure. (Now, Mahatamji paused here to mention that chronic hiccup can be quite serious, and even fatal!)

The remedy was to get sand, like from a construction site or wherever you can, and then you boil it for a time and then let it cool. Once it has cooled, you give the patient two spoonfuls of the water.

Once Malhottraji got to Delhi, he found that the man with the same post as he had, but posted in Delhi, was not to be found. This man was quite a close friend, and so Malhottraji inquired about his whereabouts, and then went to his house, but they would not let him in to see the man. Malhottraji protested, "I am his friend, tell him it is I who am here." Finally, the man relented, but Malhottraji found him in terrible shape due to unrelenting hiccups.

Malhottraji at once sent the boy of the house to fetch some sand, and, after the proper preparation, the man was cured.

Sant Gulab Singh

Sant Gulab Singh with Sripad Baba

Maharaj with Sant Gulab Singh

****

Later, in Pune, Sri Jnanananda wanted to see Rajneesh. With great anand, Sri Jnanananda mentioned the leela of Rajneesh's various names. "First," Mahatmaji said, with an assumed gravity, "he was Acharya Rajneesh. Then, he was Bhagavan Rajneesh, and it was only later that he became Osho."

"Do you know what Osho means?" Jnanananda asked. "I only know because a Japanese monk came here. It means king, like the king on the chess board. You see," He added, "Osho was like the commander of a spiritual army."

Though Jnananandaji was staying with Malhottraji, the government had forbidden its employees from seeing Osho, but Malhottraji at least consented to drive Jnananandaji to the ashram.

At the ashram, it was five Rupees for Indians, and 10 Rupees for foreigners.

As people came into the ashram, there were two women whose job it was to sniff and smell everyone. As they were smelling Him, Jnananandaji added with great anand, "Oh, we must be very fragrant!" They explained that their Guru was allergic to certain scents, and thus all the sniffing.

Once inside, there was a sign for sanyasis, and so Jnananandaji sat there, but after only a moment He was interrupted. "This is only for sanyasis," the man said. "I am a sanyasi," Jnananandaji replied. It was only for Osho sanyasis, and so the Mahatma got up and sat with the others.

Once the lecture started, many of the monks were asleep and some even snoring. Part of Osho technology was that the message might seep in during sleep.

Later, Jnananandaji came back to Malhottraji's place. "How was it?" Malhottraji asked. Jnananandaji answered, "It was worth about 10 Rupees."

The real spiritual power at that time in Pune, Mahatmaji added, was Raj Kumar Roy and Indira. That is so much like India, I thought to myself, where the real treasures are often hidden from the public eye.

✶✶✶✶✶✶✶✶✶✶✶✶✶✶✶✶

"Do not be too serious," Mahatmaji said one day, "otherwise you will be seriously ill."

✸✸✸✸✸✸✸✸✸✸✸✸✸✸✸✸✸

I laughed quite strongly at one of Jnanananda's jokes one day. "He laughs like a kriya yogi," Jnanananda said.

Later Mahatmaji added, "There are many different kinds of laughter you see," but He did not say anything more. Sometimes He left His thoughts part finished, so that the people there might work to get the real meaning of His words.

✸✸✸✸✸✸✸✸✸✸✸✸✸✸✸✸✸

The joke that had made me laugh so hard follows:

"When people used to come to see me in Mussoorie," Jnananandaji said, " I would tell them I only have two powers: either I can help you remember everything, from this life as well as from every other, or I can help you to forget."

"Everyone would choose to forget," Jnanananda said. "I would tell them you don't have to choose right now—you can sleep on it."

You see that is the punchline of the joke, although at the moment I did not grasp the meaning, so Mahatmaji quickly added, "You see everyone forgets everything when they sleep."

This brought much laughter!

✸✸✸✸✸✸✸✸✸✸✸✸✸✸✸✸✸

A group of Americans and a Frenchman came to visit Jnananandaji. After kirtan and satsang came prasad as usual. One man brought halva for everyone, but then he had to leave.

While everyone was enjoying this halva, a woman broke the silence and asked, "What made you come all the way from Switzerland to India?"

Jnananandaji pointed to His bowl with a smile and said, "I came for this!"

****

The next day, commenting on the halva incident, Jnananandaji said He had learned this from His first employer.

As a child, His Mother had taught Him well, and if He would do His prayers she would give Him a piece of chocolate.

When He grew up and someone asked Him what He wanted to do for professional life He answered simply, "Chocolate."

By "coincidence" His family was friends with a great family of chocolatiers,[47] and He was eventually able to get an internship there.

This employer taught the young man some valuable lessons, one of which was to always answer a question with the same energy that the question was asked with.

---

[47] Sprungli, who later became part of the famous Swiss brand Lindt Sprungli.

So, for an intellectual question, give an intellectual answer, and for a foolish question, give a foolish answer, and so on.

****

It was the day of the discovery of the God particle as well as the American celebration of Independence. Mahatmaji drew a parallel, "While they are celebrating Independence in America, across the world in Switzerland they are announcing the discovery of the God particle."

"Science," Mahatmaji said, "is headed in the wrong direction. Atoms, subatomic particles—if they discover that particle, they will have neither moved backward or forward.

It used to be that people lived in harmony with the earth. Rituals were done to take care of the earth, and make it a habitable place.

The scriptures of India contain all these truths. All the discoveries of science are freely displayed."

Mahatmaji then said even references to plastic bags can be found in the ancient scriptures.

Then, taking us up to the peak, He simply said, "Everything has been done."

It was a moment of deep revelation.

Everything has been done. The cycles of time and the yugas[48] go up, and they go down. We discover the God particle and think we have really gotten to a

---

[48] Cycles of time in much longer rhythms.

deeper understanding—but it does not mean a thing. Thousands of years ago, we discovered the God particle, and then we lost it. Now we are rediscovering it, and later we will lose it again and later rediscover it.

To the true lover of God (who lives in the consciousness of all those things), the rediscovery of a kind of particle can only seem like a child being given a new toy—the kind of toy the Mother is not sure if they will play with responsibly.

✳✳✳✳✳✳✳✳✳✳✳✳✳✳✳✳✳✳

Jnananandaji always said that there is a connection between certain European languages and Sanskrit. Tonight He brought up the hitchki, or hiccup, as an example, and also maakan ("anke" in Swiss German or "butter" in English). Interestingly, He said that the words relate more to a German and Swiss dialect, and less to French or Italian.

Jnananandaji was born into a world of conflict. World War II raged in His youth, and Swiss soldiers-for-hire came back with horror stories of what was happening in Germany. One Sunday, at 11am, during a church service, the whole church started shaking back and forth. Turns out, an American pilot had dropped a bomb on Switzerland thinking it was a city in Germany.

The children ran outside to the forest where the bomb had exploded, only to find furniture in the trees, with beds and dressers hanging suspended from the branches.

"When I came to my Guruji, I was a young man, 23 years old, and I had a lot of questions. There is conflict everywhere in this world. In religion there is conflict, in governments, even between spiritual organizations there is conflict. Why is there so much conflict?"

Atmananandaji simply replied, "Because everyone is right."

The young aspirant had never heard an answer like this before, and started thinking deeply.

Seeing His struggle, Atmanandaji replied, "You, also, are right!"

∗∗∗∗∗∗∗∗∗∗∗∗∗∗∗∗∗

The young aspirant once approached His Guru and asked, "Will I one day have disciples?" Atmanandaji gave a surprising reply, "Yes," He said, "but they will all be Gurus."

Once a man had approached Jnananandaji and asked if he could follow him. "Look," Jnananandaji said, "I only have one power: I can either help you to remember everything, or I can help you to forget everything."

Most people say that they would want to forget, then He smiled and looked at us all and said, "But you don't have to tell me right away."

"There was a man once who really was a disciple," Jnananandaji said. When I asked Him that question He said, "There is nothing to forget, and there is nothing to remember." This answer had deeply pleased Mahatmaji.

∗∗∗∗∗∗∗∗∗∗∗∗∗∗∗∗∗

In the above story, in a pause in the conversation, Maitreyi had commented that she had often thought there should be a third answer. Once Mahatmaji had given the answer, she said she had the same idea, and had thought the same thing. "You see," she said, "I was right."

"That leads us to another truth," Mahatamji said, "That ladies are always right."

Walking to the kitchen, Maitreyi added, "Yes, I am almost always maybe right."

✶✶✶✶✶✶✶✶✶✶✶✶✶✶✶✶✶

There was a young woman at the satsang who had known Jnananandaji since the woman had been a little child. She had lived most of her life in America, but for two weeks of every year they came back to Dehradun with the family.

The young woman had asked Mahatmaji what she should do, and, without missing a beat, He said that she should do something that had never been done before.

You have heard of the phone, and the mobile phone, but have you heard of the hriday phone? Hriday means "heart."

When Jnananandaji was young and traveling with Sri Pad, telephones were quite rare, but Sri Pad used to say why not send our calling card by thinking that we are there? Or, perhaps even better, we could go there with our hearts.

"Mail from the heart is possible," Mahatmaji said, "it

involves a certain breath control technique."

I shook my head in wonder, because Sri Jnanananda seemed to know everything about everything.

Mahatamaji then looked at me and added with a smile, "This is the kind of thing Steve loves."

****

"Yoga is concentration on the eternal, Sanatan."[49]

****

When I called Mahatmaji on the phone to ask if Sumakshi and I could visit, I had the tiniest bit of trepidation in my heart. I had come first to Jnananandaji as a young and enthusiastic Brahmachari, and now I was in a relationship. I had been with Sumakshi once before to visit Mahatmaji, and now, certainly, He would "figure it out."

After His usual Om greeting, I explained who it was that was calling, and the first words He said to me were, "Brahmachari Steve!" with great enthusiasm.

Then Sumakshi and I showed up together, and He told a story about some young Brahmacharis He had once met in India. The young man He mentioned was named Ram Das, though not the same one who is famous in America.

Ram Das had lived in India for years, and then moved back to America and married and worked as a professor at an American university. Later in the story, Mahatmaji referred to him as Brahmachari

---

[49] Sanatan means "eternal." It is often used in the context of Sanatan Dharma, the eternal Truth.

Ram Das.

Then He said about Brahmacharis, "Married or not, it does not matter."

I bowed my head in thanks for His love, big enough to hold all seekers in His light.

****

While telling the above story, we got on the subject of Ram Das, the disciple of Neem Karoli Baba. Mahatmaji said He had met Neem Karoli Baba and Bhagavan Das, who was Neem Karoli Baba's first western disciple, at Kumbh Mela[50] in Allahabad in 1965.

Mahatamji had been to the Mela with Sri Pad Baba, and I believe that is the Kumbh where Baba had his dreadlocks cut off after having been in deep samadhi for days on end.[51]

An interesting side note is that Neem Karoli Baba fed Jnanananda halva as prasaad at the Mela.

---

[50] The Kumbh Mela is a large religious fair in India that happens every 12 years.

[51] This is a story from *Transcendent Journey*. Sripad Baba was in samadhi for days and Majaraj was caring for him while the samadhi was going on. When he came out of samadhi, he asked that a photo be taken, and he offered his dreadlocks into the Ganges as an act of gratitude and devotion.

Sripad Baba

****

We were talking about Italy and the subject of Saint Francis came up. Mahatmaji stressed that Francis had owned absolutely nothing, having given everything to God. Once, he had told his disciples that he was no better than a dog. He got hold of a dog's collar and leash and had his disciples put it on him and guide him around the city of Assisi.

Later, the Pope came down hard on Francis, and, of course, eventually the order that he created relied more on money than the incredibly simple vow of poverty that Francis himself had established.

****

In the same conversation about Italy, Mahatamaji mentioned that holy basil (tulsi, in India) was engraved in certain Italian Catholic ceremonial objects (for example, it is engraved in the fount, the

95

bowl in which the baptism water is kept). Thus, the name "basil-ica." This somehow seemed to draw a connection between Francis and beloved Mother India.

✳✳✳✳✳✳✳✳✳✳✳✳✳✳✳✳

I had been with Sumakshi in Mussoorie, and she had been trying to teach me about watts and amps and the basic units of electrical equipment. I had really only listened with half of an ear, because the energy seemed a little bit off, so I was not totally focusing on the conversation.

I did wonder to myself, though, and even perhaps ask aloud to Divine Mother: what exactly am I responsible for learning in this world?

While at the Satsang, the electrician came by, but earlier in the day, Jnananandaji himself had solved the problem.

"If you are going to live in a house," He said, "you should at least know something about the water that flows into it, and the electrical and other things."

He never left even a thought unanswered.

✳✳✳✳✳✳✳✳✳✳✳✳✳✳✳✳

At one point in the Satsang, Maitreyi and a few others started to talk politics and history. As usual, I was paying more attention to attune to Sri Jnananandaji and trying to feel His inner bliss.

Then Mahatmaji said, "Do you want me to tell you something funny?"

96

"If you start to talk about politics, I will go around and put a biscuit into each one's mouth. I am completely uninterested in politics."

Having told me what we are responsible for knowing, Mahatmaji felt also to tell me what I could simply let go of.

✳✳✳✳✳✳✳✳✳✳✳✳✳✳✳✳✳

Jnananandaji went one day to a school where He had been invited to speak by the principal. He walked in, and all of the children were seated quietly in a large auditorium. As He entered, they stood to offer Him pranams.[52]

As He walked towards the children, there was a life-sized painting of Snow White and the seven dwarfs on the wall. Before He addressed the children, He went straight to the wall and offered a pranam to Snow White and the dwarfs.

"You see," He said, "most fairy tales are based upon truths from the stories of India." When the children asked about His pranam to Snow White and the dwarfs He simply replied, "I know them."

A portal was opened between Him and the children.

He remarked that the children asked very high-level questions from that moment on.

Jesus said that to come into the kingdom of God, you have to come as a child. "Children still look inwards," Mahatmaji commented, "but by the time that they are adults, they have been trained to look at the outer

---

[52] Pranams is an Indian word for "respectful greeting."

world and at externals."

During the satsang, one of the teachers tried to ask a question, but, seeing the sensitivity of the connection with the children, Mahatmaji asked that only the children be allowed to ask questions.

Later in that satsang, a young girl asked if Mahatmaji had ever seen God.

Looking at the children with love He said, "Who do you think I am speaking to right now?" The children, who are often more receptive to simple truths, clapped loudly and gave a standing ovation in celebration of this answer.

****

"Once upon a time, there was a country, but it was not any country, it was the country of all countries. And in that country, there was a city, but it was not just any city, that was the city of all cities. In that city there was a road that was the road of all roads, and on that road a house that was the house of all houses. In that house was a person. Who is that person?"

"Think deeply on this and the answer will come. It should not take a long time."

****

Mahatmaji gave a simple answer to the riddle above, so skip ahead with your eyes if you do not want to read it.

The answer is: the one (you) who is doing spiritual practice. It can be anywhere in the world.

"Guru Datattreya was a great teacher, and he was said to have twenty-four Gurus. Twenty-four was not a specific number, it was symbolic. Dattatreyaji had achieved a state where everything in creation was his Guru."

When Jnananandaji was a young man, He did an internship with a chocolatier. In those days, training in a trade was not given to just anyone. Assessment was made in terms of the character of the person. Jnananandaji also had learned from His boss as a young man. The lessons were simple, but profound. Look at the world: what to do, what not to do. That was the first lesson. Learn something new every day.

This man had also taught Jnananandaji to answer a question with the same kind of answer as the question. This made Jnanananda smile as He spoke, and certainly He is practicing this principle even today.

Jnanananda also mentioned a story from a wise man, though it was not the same chocolatier:

"If in wisdom's way you want to walk, five things observe with care: with whom you talk, of whom you talk, how, when, and where."

Imagine a world where you can learn from everything. Every leaf and every atom in creation is singing a song, but we have to learn how to listen and how to behave.

****

"Everyone you meet, you have met before."

"The Shiva lingam is symbolic of the world, and also of the inner light. Even in this world there is no such thing as darkness, there are only variations in the amount of light."

✲✲✲✲✲✲✲✲✲✲✲✲✲✲✲✲✲

Maharaj had a disciple from Princeton who came to Him with a serious medical issue. He had been to all of the doctors, but nobody could diagnose his troubles. The man was suffering from itching in the throat and a place underneath the foot.

One day they were out on a walk, and the man confessed his troubles to the Mahatma who answered, "Before I tell you the treatment, answer one question: is it your disease, or does it belong to someone else?"

Diseases can be shared. You can share a disease like you might give money to someone who needs it.

Instantly, the man recognized that the disease did not actually belong to him. He could identify two separate people to whom the disease belonged. Once there was recognition of whom the disease belonged to, the disease was gone. It was psychological.

In His kutir in Haridwar, there was a board that said of all the dharmas, compassion is the highest. One must have compassion for all the creatures of the earth. In Ayurveda, you should even be compassionate towards the disease in your body.

How different a picture this is from allopathic medicine. In Hindi, the word for pill is "goli," which is

the same word for bullet—you shoot the disease.
Where is the compassion in that?

****

In the *Bhagavad Gita*, Sri Krishna says, "Out of
thousands, only one seeks me, and out of a thousand
who seek me, only one will attain me." Mahatmaji
said that the question then is obvious: who is that
one?

The answer is "you."

The *Gita* was meant to be transmitted from Guru to
disciple.

****

"Truth is beneficial, Truth protects."

Mahatmaji had a book on His table called *Sacred
Animals of India.* Commenting on the book one day,
He said that, "Dogs accompany the Goddess of
healing."

"In Assyrian buildings the dogs would flank the
entrance as protectors."

****

Commenting about the Christmas tree, Mahatmaji
once said, "Why do you first kill the tree, then
decorate it and only then worship it?" The decorating
of the tree came from the Indian custom of Rakhi,
where people would tie rakhis on deodar trees for
protection. Deodar means "tree of the Gods." This
kind of tree can be found in Mussoorie.

Many people around the world are finding India. When He was a young man, Jnananandaji said He met a village elder. The young Jnanananda told the man He wanted to travel, and the man, though unlearned, said that everywhere is the same. Everywhere there is the same sun and moon, and the same stars. He was telling Jnananandaji that everything is inside.

Everywhere you go, you end up surrounded by the same sort of people. In Kolkata, perhaps they have a different color skin. Everyone is in everything. That means if you hate someone, you hate not only everything on this planet, but everything in the universe. Everything is interconnected.

****

It was in a Kerala ashram in the 1960s when Maharaj first felt He should write His own chants. The first chant that He wrote was Ananda Brahma. In a different satsang, Mahatmaji had mentioned that Ananda Brahma was the chant of creation, the beginning of the Cosmic Motion Picture show, as Om began the dance of creation.

****

Mahatmaji was once talking about sadhus, and the life of wandering in search of the Divine. Mahatmaji mentioned that He Himself was a sadhu, and that only a sadhu can recognize a sadhu. "You can recognize them by looking in the eyes," He said. At some point in the story I laughed and then Jnananandaji said, "Steve is the laughing sadhu." Then, once again, He repeated that only a sadhu can recognize a sadhu, and that the eyes never change from lifetime to lifetime.

Yogananda's brother's son-in-law gave Mahatmaji a photo of Badri Narayan in Badrinath Temple in India, taken in 1946. The name of the young man that took the photograph was Buddha Bose. Before photographs were common in India, he had come to the temple in the early morning and snapped a shot of Badri Narayan. Later, Buddha Bose had that photograph blown up and used to meditate in front of it.

Jnananandaji Himself had a copy of that photo, and He shared it with a French woman who was a sculptor living in India. Her name was Florence Rastogi, and she was the director of a college of art. As she made the sculpture of Babaji, she learned something. She said the sculpture was neither male nor female, and it is Nar and Nareshwar, which is to say both God and man.

Later, Mahatmaji added that "Nar" is also close to the word for water (nir) in Sanskrit.

Mahatmaji often referred to Sumakshi and I as birds. In fact, the first time we came to the kutir together, He said, "Look, the song birds have come."

We were visiting the Mahatma before Sumakshi and I were to leave on a trip to America. At the end of the satsang, Mahatmaji said, "Today these people will become birds and fly to America."

One day when I was particularly tired, the Maharaj, seeing my state, simply commented, "Steve needs a chai!"

✶✶✶✶✶✶✶✶✶✶✶✶✶✶✶✶✶

We were talking one day about the book *The Little Prince.* In that discussion, Mahatmaji said, "I am the little prince from another planet."

✶✶✶✶✶✶✶✶✶✶✶✶✶✶✶✶✶

"There was a Mahatma who would sit to drink a cup of tea with you, and he could tell you your past, present, and future."

Mahatmaji then looked at Sumakshi and said, "Are you sure you still want chai?"

✶✶✶✶✶✶✶✶✶✶✶✶✶✶✶✶✶

Once, Maharaj had a group of 35 people from Europe coming, and so when Sumakshi and I called Him to ask what time to come, He said, "Come immediately!"

At the door of His campsite, Jnananandaji greeted Sumakshi and I by saying, "The early birds have arrived!" It was raining, and hail was coming, and He said, "And you have brought the rain and hail with you."

Once we came in, He said in His impish way, "Come have a seat, and I will tell you a story you have never heard before."

"A young man came to visit me, he worked for the forest service, as an environmentalist, and he asked me what kind of food I like. Without thinking, I answered, 'I like to eat the kind of food that likes me.'"

The young man had a keen wit, and he smiled with understanding.

Mahatmaji added, "This is very important. Many people like the food that does not like them! One must be careful!"

Later, a group of American and Colombian ladies came to visit, and the Mahatmaji was teasing them before they entered the door. "Everyone that comes through that door becomes old." They all looked at the door, hesitating to enter. "The soul," Mahatmaji added, "is ancient." With that comment, they relaxed and understood that He was only joking with them.

With this same group of older ladies, Mahatmaji had told the story of the environmentalist, and then gave them all a biscuit. (It was Mahatmaji's habit to give out prasad in the form of a biscuit and tea to guests before the satsang. He would often take one as well.)

At one point, Mahatmaji looked down at the biscuit in His hand and said, "Do you like me?"

The women smiled, but Mahatmaji felt more was needed. He looked at the biscuit again and said sweetly, "Do you love me?"

The group of women burst out laughing.

****

Raksha Bandhan is a festival in India which literally translates into "Band of Protection." Rakhi, as it is also called, is known as the time in India where sisters tie a Rakhi on their brother's wrist. The tie is a symbol of the sister's love and prayers for the brother, and a symbol that the brother will vow to protect the sister.

The Mahatma often used to take a little trek[53] into the forest in the afternoons. There was a very quiet place, with very few people and very little traffic, but a lot of trees and the spacious beauty of Mother Nature. On this walk, Mahatmaji had tied rakhis to many of the trees.

In parts of India, rakhis are still tied to trees to symbolize that Nature can protect mankind if mankind, in turn, gives love to Mother Nature and all her creatures and forms.

On this walk Jnanananda used to collect the flowers that had fallen to the forest floor. "In the forest," He would say, "they look quite sad, lying there and wilting." He would take them home and place them in water and they would come back to life. These were beautiful, big, yellow flowers.

He would talk with the trees and the flowers as He walked, and they were very much His friends.

One day, He was walking in the forest where He met a man with a motorcycle. The man looked quite unlike the quiet, serene forest, with the birds and the flowers and trees all singing.

The man spoke to the Mahatmaji and said, "Who are you?"

Mahatmaji answered and then the man asked, "Where do you live?" The Mahatma told the man where He lived.

Then the man asked, "Are you renting?"

"Yes," the Mahatma answered, "I am. Sometimes there is a headache, sometimes a pain in the leg."

The man did not realize that the Mahatma was talking about the rent He paid for this body. For His campsite (He never referred to the house as His, He always said, "I am camping here.") He paid nothing, except the blessings we all experienced while being in His presence.

****

After talking about the forest and the trees, Mahatmaji added, "The first step in Self-realization is that you begin to see yourself in everything."

****

Sumakshi and I arrived in town, and I called Jnananandaji on the phone, very much looking forward to His ever-new greeting, which, inevitably, was filled with some variety of Om. Sometimes Hari Om, or Om Om. Many other variations were also there.

"How many of you are coming?" the Mahatmaji asked. I answered that Sumakshi and I were both coming.

"Ahhhh," He replied, "there are two of you. One plus one equals eleven. There is a big group coming tonight, forty people, but I think I can squeeze you in."

When we arrived, He said, "The early birds are here. I have a spot of tea for you. Have it quickly before the group gets here—I can't make chai for such a big group."

Later in the satsang, He said a children's rhyme I had never heard Him say before:

"Tick-tick-tick says the clock. Whatever you do, do it quick."

The Maharaj once visited a saint named Sharir Maharaj, who spoke to Him in jumbled Hindi that nobody there understood, except the one whom it was intended for. Later, Asangananada asked Sri Pad Baba, and Baba confirmed the exact meaning that the Maharaj had understood.

Similarly, this statement was a strange one. I do feel like it was intended for Sumakshi and I. Later when we spoke, we both confirmed the same meaning from what seemed like a meaningless childhood rhyme shared in fun. For personal reasons, though, the meaning must remain a secret.

Gyanamata, the most advanced woman disciple of Paramhansa Yogananda, once said that even when the Master made what seemed like a mistake, it paid to listen attentively to His words.

This little children's rhyme was one of the greatest gifts ever given to me by Jnanananda.

Still, it made me see that every Word from a man of God is prasad. Each little word is a gift.

****

"There are some Gurus coming today," Mahatmaji said with a grin, "'Internet Gurus.' One should not say that and make fun, but," and He smiled with a little giggle, "there are many Gurus these days. Many Gurus but not many disciples."

"Are there many true Gurus?" Sumakshi asked.

"Everyone is a true Guru," He replied. "I have written it in my book. You see, everyone gets the Guru they deserve."

Later, before the others came, He said to us, "Let us have some fun. When they ask you who you are, you can say that you are Gurus, and that you have come from the Moon."

Later in the satsang, a woman leaned over and asked me where Sumakshi and I were from. Remembering the Maharaj's words I replied, "We are Gurus. We have come from the Moon."

The woman smiled in a shy sort of way, and then replied, "Well, I have never met such a one before, so I have no way of telling if what you say is true."

✱✱✱✱✱✱✱✱✱✱✱✱✱✱✱✱✱

"I have a devotee in Columbia, and her daughter is the one that painted this picture." The Mahatma pointed to a beautiful forest landscape that He kept on the table near His harmonium. "She is twenty-three."

Picking up the picture, He turned it over, where there was a letter from the young woman. The words of the letter were exquisitely expressed and the sentiment quite lovely. I do not remember the exact words, unfortunately, but the sentiment was that humanity had forgotten how to love this planet, and the planet needs and wants our love.

Jnananandaji sent word through her mother that she should write a biography of how other species see humans. She could start with the animals. How dogs see humans. How horses see humans. Then the plants, and the trees, and the rocks. Then, later, the five elements—how the five elements see humans.

Just after He had sent this message to Manuella (the young painter), He found an African proverb in the newspaper. He had the clipping of that proverb tucked in His copy of *Transcendent Journey*. It said:

"Until lions have their historians, tales of the hunt shall always glorify the hunter."

"Isn't this interesting? Will you send this to her?"

Later, it did occur to me that Maharaj had often referred to himself as a lion. It did also occur to me that, perhaps by God's grace, I may function, along with many others, in part, as that lion's historian. Perhaps that is why He gave the article to Sumakshi and I to send.

****

"Sumakshi is very sharp. She gets everything. She is an artist."

****

When Mahatmaji got to India, He had with Him a Swiss watch in His possession. Upon arrival in India, He gave it to an elderly sadhu in Haradwar.

"I told myself, 'I am in India now. I don't need it.'"

"I can close my eyes and visualize any clock—like the clock on a cathedral in Switzerland, or even the face of a wrist watch—and I can see the time."

"Now," the Mahatmaji added with a smile, "I keep watch."

****

I have a friend in Mussoorie. He had read *Autobiography of a Yogi* in three months. I gave him my book. When he met me, he said, "Swamiji, I can't put it down."

"You should read the book until the book reads you. I told this to an old man and he was able to tell me exactly what page, which part of the book, this is in. No one else has been able to tell me that."

"Holy books can read you—scriptures and things like that. Try it. When you are having a problem, hold it in your mind and just open the book. It will respond to you."

"I had four people come to visit me recently. They had just come from Ramakrishna Mission, and they had some leaflets to give me. When they arrived, I asked them to read at random from *Transcendent Journey*."

The first opened to the part where Ramakrishna and Sarada Devi appear to me at Dakshineswar. They, of course, had just come from the Ramakrishna mission.

The second opened to the part where money in the book is described as worthless bits of paper. It was from the time when German currency had undergone huge inflation, and the young Asangananda was surprised to find bills worth as much as 100,000 marks in the drawer of a desk. His Mother informed him that they were now "worthless pieces of paper." Jnananandaji hinted that this man was "overly concerned with money."

The third man opened to the page where the Pilgrim had lost 10 kilos of weight. Swamiji, with a smile, commented that this man was perhaps concerned with his weight.

The next man opened to the pages in the book which describe the diamond mines of Panna. Panna is famous for the only diamonds in the world that lie close to the Earth's surface. Strangely, this man admitted that he had been counting his family's jewelry before he came.

Books are not books. A book written by a saint is a passageway, and it can lead you to your own true Self.

✸✸✸✸✸✸✸✸✸✸✸✸✸✸✸✸

"My Mother would get me to pray to my Guardian Angel when I was little. This makes more sense to children than praying to God. She would put a piece of chocolate in my mouth and make me pray, and I grew to love chocolate. Mothers are very smart!"

✸✸✸✸✸✸✸✸✸✸✸✸✸✸✸✸

Some communist government officials had come to see Jnananandaji in Mussoorie. They loved the trees and the beauty of nature there. They were from the planning commission, and so they had this question, "How do you make your living?"

Mahatmaji simply replied, "I have a pension."

They shook their heads and then paused and asked, "Where is the pension from?"

"From God." And He pointed upwards.

"But we do not believe in God. We are communists."

"It does not matter if you believe in God or not, still, He is the One that is giving me my pension."

Later, they changed their beliefs and left the Communist Party.

****

One day, Jnanananda started into the topic of sports. "Soccer," He said with great enthusiasm and a pause... "It is very interesting. It tells you about the people. In soccer they want to kick the ball. Or hit it. They want to beat it up. Other sports, you want to throw the ball. I once asked Maitreyi's Mom about cricket and she replied, 'Angrezi Raj.'"[54]

"I went to a cricket game once, in England, with a friend. I had been there and one hour passed, and then two hours passed, then a third went by. 'How long before the game ends?'" the young Asangananada asked his friend. The reply, "Tomorrow afternoon."

"That was it. I left, and I have never been to a game again."

"These things are a kind of hypnotism."

---

[54] Angrezi Raj translates roughly to "British rule," as in "British rule over India."

****

There was a Swamiji who called me to ask me for my mobile number. "Mere pas nehi hai, landline baba hoon." (Translation: I do not have one, I am a landline, Baba!)

"You see I have three numbers, and there are three types of telephones. There is the phone number of bhootkal—the past. 'Bhoot' is a ghost. You can learn many things from Hindi. This [using the phone number to the past] you can never do without the permission of the Guru."

When Mahatmaji was a young man He stayed in Lahore, and there He played a game with someone where you could invoke a soul to ask it questions. He chose to invoke Paramhansa Yogananda, who promptly appeared, and then scolded the young man for calling upon him in a game. Thus with the past, the Mahatma advised leaving it alone unless you had the permission of the Guru.

The other is vartaman, the present, and the third is bhaviṣya, the future. The future will reveal itself to you at appropriate moments, as needed. You cannot force it, though. It will reveal itself only as needed.

The next day, we asked Mahatmaji about the present telephone, but He just laughed.

The present is a gift, and it is also eternal.

****

There was a large group coming with the Internet Gurus mentioned above. Just before the group came, Jnananandaji said, "Now you will see a theater."

The group was from Spain. Amongst the group there were six different languages. "They cannot sing," Mahatmaji commented, "because they can't agree on a language."

Only humans have speech, everything else sings. Every atom sings. They sing mantras.

The Bible talks about only one language in the beginning. The language of the heart. Telepathy. A yogi can communicate from here to America without the help of a cell phone.

Sanskrit was the first written language. It is not man-made. It came from inside. (He pointed to the spine.) There is a Sanskrit letter on each petal of each chakra. A side effect of kriya yoga is that each of the petals begins to vibrate, and the sound can be heard in deep meditation.

****

In His leela, Sri Jnanananda had come up with certain therapies to help maintain health. There was, of course, the previously mentioned "baby yoga therapy" (with Dhirananda from YSS who, coincidentally, had special training in the yoga postures).

There was the aforementioned "tree therapy," which it turns out was well loved by Vidura from Ananda, who used to lead pilgrimage groups to India.

Then there was "Langoor therapy." Maharaj had noticed that monkeys hang on the tree with their arms and simultaneously lift up their legs. He mentioned that somehow this eases the strain on the back. To hang on something and lift the legs is excellent for the health of the spine.

Then, of course, there was "gratitude therapy". Gratitude to the body leads to the greatest health.

✱✱✱✱✱✱✱✱✱✱✱✱✱✱✱✱

In addition to the Guru industry, Mahatmaji said there is the Yoga industry, and even the ashram industry! Maharaj told us the following story to illustrate His point:

A man came here and asked, "How many guest rooms do you have?"

"Guest rooms," Jnananandaji replied, "I do not even have a room for myself! I sleep here." (And He pointed to the asan[55] where He played music.)

They never came back.

✱✱✱✱✱✱✱✱✱✱✱✱✱✱✱✱

Sumakshi pointed out an All Out (a ball that repels mosquitoes) that was not plugged in. "Oh!" Mahatmaji replied, "They forgot to use it!"

"They never bother me," He said about the mosquitoes. "They used to just come on me and walk on my arm, but never actually bite."

When the Mahatma was a young man, He encountered mosquitoes first in Italy. At that point

---

[55] An asan is a thin mat.

He was bitten, but, later, by His Guru's grace, they did not bite Him anymore.

"When I was with Swami Krishnanandaji they all used to go to him. He used to say that it was because his blood was sweet." Then Krishnananda would look at Jnananandaji and say, "Your blood is bitter."

"Otherwise, mosquitos can be quite terrible!" And the Mahatma made a face of comic dismay, followed by one of His big, beautiful, contagious smiles.

****

I knew a sadhu who was silent for four months of the monsoon and two of the winter. He was living near me in Mussoorie, but he never came to visit me.

I told people who went to visit him that if he does not speak, you mustn't either, and if he writes, then you should write. Otherwise it is rude, don't you think?

There was a moment of silence, and the Mahatmaji added, "Of course some people feel that not talking is rude!" This evoked from the group a gentle laugh.

From the perspective of a yogi, it is difficult to get everything just right in this world.

****

Once, the Mahatma was walking on the mall road in Shimla, and someone said to Him, "The world is coming to an end."

The Mahatma calmly responded, "I thought it had already ended."

The true Sanyasi is dead to the world.

****

"In India, it is not enough to take precaution, you have to be immune."

****

Once, the Mahatma was undergoing a pain in the back. He had even gone to the chemist to get pills for the pain.

He had been with that pain for some time, when, one night, He approached His bed. It was the habit of the Mahatma to sleep in the temple where He used to give satsang. He would lay out an asan and pillow for Himself and another asan for Dharma, and there they would sleep side-by-side.

But this night He came back and found Dharma the dog already asleep in His bed. Jagjivan Babu had taught Him never to disrupt anything, not even in animals. So He left Dharma there in His bed. Dharma had even put his head on the Mahatma's pillow. So Mahatmaji took a pillow from the corner, and He, Himself, lay down on Dharma's asan to sleep.

The next day when He woke up, all of the back pain was gone. From that night onwards, He slept on Dharma's bed and Dharma slept on what used to be Mahatmaji's bed.

Mahatmaji had those pills from the chemist still lying unused, because the pain had been taken away.

Much later, five days before Dharma passed away, the pain in Mahatmaji's back strangely returned. They knew that Dharma was very close to passing on.

While narrating the story, Mahatmaji explained that when people pass on, they begin to withdraw their prana well before the body dies. This process of withdrawal of the prana can take days, Mahatmaji said.

Then, one night, Maitreyi and Jnananandaji knew that the time was close. The Mahatma was sitting under a tree for meditation, and Dharma began to bark like he had never barked before. It was so loud and powerful that Maitreyi thought that another dog had come into the house. His whole life he had never barked like that, with so much power and force. It was his way of saying farewell.

Mahatmaji came in later and took the dog from his bed and held him on His lap to comfort him. Two old friends, sharing the last moments of life together.

By this time, it was late at night, close to 1am, and Maitreyi came to take Dharma so that Mahatmaji could sleep. As she took the dog, she heard a deep grumbling sound. She knew that sound was his last breath, but did not want to tell Jnananandaji, and so she carried him over to his bed, and a few minutes later they both realized that he had passed on.

After the night of Dharmaji's passing, the Mahatma's back pain left again, never to return. The Mahatma still sleeps on the bed of a dog-that-was-not-really-a-dog. A friend in life, and a friend in death, and a loyal and true companion even after death.

****

The Mahatma had a gurubhai[56] who was an eccentric Finnish painter. This man lived for a time in his car, at another time in a boat, and, once, actually drove from Finland to India by car.

When that man came to the abode of the Mahatma, he asked gruffly, "Why do you keep a dog?" And then he disapprovingly looked at Dharma.

The Mahatma simply replied, "He is here to serve a purpose."

"What purpose?" the painter replied.

"To keep people away."

At this point in the story the Mahatma started laughing gently and added, "Then the man understood and started liking Dharma. You see, they became friends because they recognized each other!"

✱✱✱✱✱✱✱✱✱✱✱✱✱✱✱✱✱

The Mahatma often spoke of what He called the "comercianalization" of knowledge. (And yes, He did actually pronounce the "n," which looks like a typo!) Asangananda had said that knowledge was the fruit from the tree of life, and that it should be shared freely. Nothing could be bought at the Mahatma's satsang, everything, including His CDs and books and poetry, were given as prasad to the right person at the right time.

That particular day, someone had called from Romania asking to translate *Transcendent Journey*

---

[56] Gurubhai literally means "brother" or "sister" of the same Guru. It refers to someone who has the same spiritual teacher as you.

into Romanian. Many others had asked to participate in some way.

The Mahatma was always welcoming of such ideas, but He would make it clear that He did not give initiations, and sales were the furthest thing from His mind, because all that He had was shared freely with all.

He did mention in this satsang, that in the Switzerland of old, you did not take on an apprentice until you had assessed the man's character. "That," Mahatmaji said, "is the problem today."

A local Swami had claimed to be initiated by the Mahatma. Asangananda, with a smile, called it an "outright lie."

This Swami had dealings with the mafia, and fundraised on the Internet. These activities were foreign to the true renunciate, who shared wisdom freely with all—even the trees and the flowers on His daily walk!

✳✳✳✳✳✳✳✳✳✳✳✳✳✳✳✳✳

There is a cave in the Himalayas, known as Vashista Gufa, or more literally "the cave of Vashista," who was the Guru of Ram and one of the Saptarishis.[57]

In His youth, of course, Sri Jnananandaji wandered often in the Himalayas. Not only did He know that cave, but He had spent a lot of time with the Mahatmas that stayed there, and that topic is well covered in *Transcendent Journey*.

---

[57] Saptarishis are seven great Rishis, or Sages, of India.

One day in Satsang, we were talking about the cave, and the Mahatma made the following comments:

Apparently, Lord Ram had asked sage Vashista where he had been in his previous life, and the sage showed him. Curiously enough, the event from the previous life had taken place right in the very same room in which they were sitting, off to the side, in a corner of the room. Then the Mahatma mentioned His own relationship to that wonderful place.

"I have not been to that cave since 1961," He said, "That was when I realized that the cave was inside of me."

****

In His youth in Switzerland, women were not allowed to vote. "Only those," Jnanananda said, "who carried a sword had the right to vote."

Of course carrying a sword was not a literal thing, it was a reference to those who would fight to defend the country.

"Politics, even then, was considered a dirty thing and not fit for women." Then, with a laugh, He added, "Of course women did most of the voting anyways. They were at home telling the husbands which one to vote for!"

In those days there was no Internet or TV, and most of the news was spread by women. They would meet on the street corner and talk, and news generally circulated this way.

The Mahatma then paused to say, "In any case, ladies are always right. Especially Mothers. Mothers are always right!

On the topic of the common man, the Mahatma related a story—told to Him by Anandamayi Ma—of a king who had been searching for answers to a few simple questions. Unfortunately, nobody seemed to be able to answer those simple questions.

The questions were:

> What does God eat?
> When does God weep?
> What makes God laugh?
> What is God doing?

A peasant, hearing this, said, "That is easy. I can answer this. Take me to the King."

Though every scholar and brain in the kingdom was searching for the answer, this peasant claimed to know.

So the king asked, "What does God eat?"

The young man answered, "The ego."

Quite impressed, the king asked the next question, "Why does God weep?"

"Because we have forgotten Him," the peasant replied.

"Then when does God laugh?"

"When we say 'I own this land, or I cured this person.'," replied the young man.

Suitably impressed, the king ventured forth his last question, "Then," he said, "what is God doing?"

For this question, the peasant was not so quick to answer and appeared to hesitate a moment. The king, of course, demanded an answer.

"For that," the young man said, "you and I will have to exchange places."

Looking somewhat displeased, the king removed himself from the throne, and walked out into the audience. The young peasant walked up to the throne, and sat quietly for a moment, and then replied, "This is what he does!"

****

When Maharaj was a young man, He was in England working as a chocolatier. On a trip back to Switzerland, He was visiting an aunt who was a vegetarian and was secretly practicing yoga.

At that time, vegetarianism in Switzerland was almost unheard of, but this aunt would simply say that the doctor had told her something and then people would let her be.

On the 7th of March, 1952, the Mahatma's aunt gave Him a gift that would change His life forever. It was a copy of the book *Autobiography of a Yogi*, by Paramhansa Yogananda (given on the exact day of the Master's passing from this earth).

Immediately, the young man wanted to go to India, but His friends counseled otherwise. "Why not go to America?" they asked.

"The sun right now is setting in America," the young man replied, "and it is rising over India."

Three months later, the young man left for India on foot, alone.

★★★★★★★★★★★★★★★★

When Jnanananda was a child, He had quite a sense of adventure. One day, He got 15 or 16 of His friends together to conduct an experiment. Once they were gathered, He announced the day's events: they were all to go out begging.

At first, the children were incredulous. Nobody begs in Switzerland, they protested. (They were all from good families.) Nevertheless, Jnananandaji was magnetic, and very persuasive, and so the group all set out on their new adventure.

Begging, like anything else in life, is an art. The true beggar will only beg alone, and never in a group. "When you see a group of beggars," Mahatmaji added, "they are amateurs. If she has to, of course, a woman can beg with a child. Other than that, you have to beg alone."

"I have learned many things from beggars," Mahatmaji said. "My song, Sri Ram Jai Ram, came from a beggar on the train. This young man was perfectly healthy, but would walk up and down the train singing bhajans and begging for money. This was a long time ago. You do not see this type of thing much anymore."

Another young man walked around Mahatmaji's neighborhood, and everyone in the neighborhood thought he was crazy. As he walked, the young man used to count, but Mahatmaji informed us that he never counted the number eight.

"Everyone thought he was crazy," Mahatmaji said, "but I could see something different."

"The number nine is Brahmaswarup.[58] Multiply any number with nine, and what do you get? Still you have nine. Nine times seven, is sixty-three, and six plus three equals nine. Eight is Mayaswarup. Multiply eight and every number becomes smaller when reduced to the single digit. Eight times six equals forty-eight, and four plus eight equals twelve, then one plus two equals three which is smaller than eight. Or eight times seven equals fifty-six, and five plus six equals eleven, and one plus one is two. In the case of eight, there are diminishing returns—thus the name Mayaswarup!"

The day before, in a magical moment, Sumakshi and I had seen nine birds. Both of us were curious about the meaning of the number nine. Interestingly, a group had come that night: nine Russians.

Once, a begging Swami had come to the door, and he complained that he had not been given enough. "I am going to Haradwar." The young man everyone thought was mad, who never counted eight, came running over. His comment: "You have to go to Haradwar everyday?"

Somehow that young man knew that this beggar was a fake, and somehow he knew that the number eight just doesn't add up!

---

[58] Brahmaswarup means "like Brahma," or "the essence of Brahma." So, Mayaswarup would mean "the essence of Maya." Maya is the measurer or delusion. That which gives the illusion that the One is separate.

****

Once, at a satsang, a businessperson from Russia came. Coincidentally, on the same day, another businessperson was also there. They had heard of breathlessness, and they had heard that a certain power, or siddhi, came when you were in this breathless state.

"Can you show us how to achieve this breathless state?" they asked.

"Oh," Mahatmaji replied, "I am too old to show you that sort of thing, but I will tell you an interesting story."

"The minute I entered India, I entered the breathless state. I realized that breath was not my breath, but it was God's breath passing through me. The Bible itself says that God breathed life into mankind."

The subject of the breath brought the Mahatma to the ancient technique of kriya yoga.

"There are many kinds of kriya," Mahatmaji said. "Kriya is anything that takes someone toward God. Anandamayi Ma, in her book, describes thousands of kriyas."

"Once, I was at Lahiri Mahashaya's house in Benares. You used to be able to enter freely, but now they have it locked up. My Guru was there, and we were talking with his son about kriya. Someone asked, 'In kriya do you breathe with the mouth open, or closed and through the nose?' Mahashaya's son answered, 'Neither.'" At that moment Jnanananda looked at His Guru, who smiled and nodded.

Mahatmaji did not add more here, but He hinted that each Master has the right to change and adjust the techniques. Then He added that He Himself had added something to the ancient practice of kriya.

"I have added something to the science of kriya yoga," Mahatmaji said, "Be thankful for the breath."

∗∗∗∗∗∗∗∗∗∗∗∗∗∗∗∗∗

When Mahatmaji was a child, His Mother had a book with a picture of Rodin's "Thinker" on the cover.

"I was a very curious child," He said, "and I was interested, but I would NOT open that book. I did not understand why, but I did not want to open it."

On the altar, Mahatmaji had a Ganesha sculpture in a similar pose to Rodin's famous "Thinker."

"Now, look at the Ganesha on the altar. He has his left hand pressing into his left jaw in contemplation. A Westerner would never have made that."

Mahatmaji left us to consider that for a moment and then added, "They have discovered that the right brain is more spiritual and the left brain is more of this world. When you press something on the left side. you stimulate the right brain, and when you press on the right side, you stimulate the left."

This story touches on so many levels, but, most of all, it left me with the feeling that we understand so little. Every gesture, every moment affects us, and yet even the most simple of gestures is not understood.

The altar

****

One night, Jnanananda was expecting a group from Russia. They were supposed to arrive at 4:30pm from Rishikesh, although I have a feeling He knew it would not work out that way because He asked us to come after 5pm. Sure enough, they were caught in a traffic jam. After waiting some time, Jnananandaji asked

Vinod to make Him some chai, and added that Vinod ought to make some for himself.

"One must never eat alone," He said, and then paused. "Oh yes, even in the *Bhagavad Gita* it is written. To eat alone is a sin. One must always share their food. If nobody is around to share with, then you can share with the birds, or the dogs, or cows, but one must certainly share."

Strangely, the Mahatma had never mentioned this to me before, and it was not until I was there with Sumakshi that it was mentioned.

This confirmed an inner feeling that Sumakshi had always had, that Maharaj had beautifully brought to light. It had been a slight point of contention in our relationship, and the Mahatma had ironed out that misunderstanding with a few well-spoken words.

Every thought, and everything one wondered about, however small, was answered by the Master from the Himalayas.

****

The same day that the Russians came, Jnananandaji revealed a very interesting aspect of His personality. The Mahatma always began His chanting promptly at sandhya kal,[59] which is a time of great spiritual power. Maharaj had asked the group to come at that time, but, due to certain circumstances, they had arrived over two hours late.

Mahatmaji was in His eighties at this time, and it would have been well within His rights to express

---

[59] Sandyha is the twilight hour. Sandhya literally means "bridge," and Kal means "time."

some discontent with this inconvenience, but the Mahatma did not even mention it. He greeted everyone with His customary joy and hospitality.

"I am going to sing now," He said. "Singing is free! Speaking is very costly! Human beings are the only ones who speak. Speaking is a degradation of language! Isn't that a strange thing? Nature sings. All of Nature is singing a song, a mantra. Even the atoms are singing. By the practice of kriya you can hear the sound of the atoms."

Later in the same satsang, Jnananandaji talked about mantras. "You have to chant the mantra until the mantra chants you," He said. "You have to learn to listen to the mantra. If you are still chanting the mantra, you have a long way to go. Each one has a mantra, but we have to learn to hear it."

****

When the Russians came, Jnananandaji talked about love and the role of the heart in yoga.

Sri Jnanananda mentioned a disciple named V P Singh. Mahatmaji gave him the spiritual name Vardhananada. Speaking about him, Mahatmaji said, "He is one of the only people we let stay here at the house. He was a very spiritual man. He did not marry. Later in his life he developed a heart problem." Mahatmaji said to him, "You did not give your heart to anyone."

****

"To do yoga, you have to listen, and you have to think."

"Think," Mahatmaji pointed at His head.

First, listen and think, and then meditate and focus on the heart.

Jnanananda once knew a royal family, and was speaking to them about love and, more specifically, the stages of love.

"First, you hear about love," He said, "and then you begin to think about love. Then the third stage is that you fall in love." He paused. "Then you have to become love."

At this point, the daughter of the royal family took out a small piece of paper that she had tucked into her shirt, near her heart. It was a note that she had been given by her Guru, and it said, "Be love."

The daughter said to Jnananandaji that she had never understood the words of her Guru until Jnananandaji had clarified them for her.

****

Jnananandaji was reminiscing one day about our early meetings. "When Steve first came here," He said, "he asked me if I cut my hair."

I must have had an incredulous look, and, catching my thought, He said, "Oh yes—you do not remember?"

"Of course I do not even look in the mirror, or cut my hair, but, ever since, Steve leaves money here when he leaves. He is afraid I will not have money for a haircut," and with this punchline Jnananandaji chuckled.

It was a strange moment with Mahatmaji, and, like everything He said, I am sure it is true on many levels, and yet I think it was His simple way of saying, "You are family and you do not need to leave me money." Strangely, though, I never could leave without placing something on the magical wooden sandals neatly placed near the altar. He gave so much and never asked anything at all in return. Truly He was the embodiment of Christs' words, "It is more blessed to give than to receive."

****

When I met Maharaj at the gate I asked him, "How are you, Swamiji?"

He answered, "I am."

****

"Ok! Enough of talking! Now singing. As long as one sings, they don't grow old! My Guru said when He stopped singing, He would stop living."

****

The name Einstein means "one stone" in German. During those days, many German Jews were changing their names. Einstein was trying to find the smallest particle, and he, or perhaps his father, gave their family this name.

Einstein also knew of reincarnation. "Oh yes, he had some idea of these things. I read once a quote of his in the vairagya patr."[60] The Mahatma then paused to explain, "You see," He said, "when you read the newspaper, you want to leave the world!" And we all laughed.

The essence of the quote was:

If I ever come back again, I will not come as a scientist.

"You see he could see the direction that science was going. He would prefer even to be a plumber. When I was a child we saw videos of the atom bombs in Nagasaki. People were melting into sidewalks. Can you imagine such a thing? These things happen on this planet.

Einstein said something that surprised me so much, I was amazed when I read about it. They asked him about his entering space, and he said 'I entered it when I was a child.' You cannot enter it as an adult. Still, every child has that ability. Only we forget as adults."

"As adults, we look at things," and He touched the harmonium, "but we do not see the things that are in between."

✶✶✶✶✶✶✶✶✶✶✶✶✶✶✶✶

"There is a ruin, a khandar,[61] in the forest where I take my walk. That forest belongs to the military. Someone saw me walking there once and asked what I was doing, and I said I was the police." The Mahatma,

---

[60] Vairagya means "detachment." Patr means "paper." It could be translated as the paper that causes detachment. It is how Maharaj used to refer to the newspaper.

[61] Khandar means a "ruin" in Urdu.

with great emphasis, then added, "The spiritual police!" And we all laughed. "I learned this thing," He added, "from Sri Pad Baba!"

While we were there that night, Mahatmaji took a phone call from the General responsible for this military area. The General himself had gone to inspect what the Mahatmaji had called one of the "Wonders of India."

The wonder was an old ruin with three doors that always had been shut. "When I would walk there, I would always feel a great attraction to the building, but since the doors were closed, I just kept walking."

One day, one of the doors stood open, and the Mahatmaji entered to find a large room (about three times the size of His satsang room, but square and with four large pillars).

"I immediately chanted Om, and the sound came back 'Hhrrrrooooom!' That sound almost went up my spine!

Soon after, I brought Gangajal[62] to the room, and then later put flowers there."

"I had seen something like that once before—at the Taj Mahal in Agra. I was staying with the caretaker of the Taj Mahal and the red fort, and he showed me things that can no longer be shown to the public, because of government orders. There are seven stories to the Taj Mahal. Inside, there is a chamber that can also be used for chanting Sanskrit mantras. You see, the Taj used to be a Shiva temple.[63]

---

[62] Gangajal is water from the sacred Ganges River.

[63] The name Teja Mahalaya: Tej for "Shiva" or "light," and Mahalaya translates as the "Great Abode."

In any case, that ruin in the forest was considered by a living saint to be excellent for chanting in Sanskrit. You could say 'Brahmanandam,' or 'Om, Tat, Sat.'" It was a stormy night, and just after Mahatmaji said "Sat" came a loud clap of thunder that seemed to accentuate His words.

All of Nature is in symphony with He that knows He is in everything!

****

"Nowhere will you hear stories like the stories that you hear here."

****

"The secret of prasad," Mahahtmaji said one day, "the rishis of old knew. Even when you are chanting or meditating, your mind is wandering. Hanuman Poddar, of Gita Press said, 'If you think of Vrindavan, then you are in Vrindavan.' If you are in Vrindavan, and you are thinking about Dehradun, then you are in Dehradun. If, in your mind, you are in America, or Italy, or Pune, then you are there. The mind is always wavering. The rishis of old knew this. But when prasad comes out," He made a gesture of focus with His hand, "there is focus—total concentration... What has arrived for prasad today?"

****

One night, Jnananandaji made a joke, and then looked at one of the Brahmacharis and commented:

_____

"Bara laughs with one eye. Maybe the other eye is
looking at his chai!" At that point, Bara himself
started laughing again, and Mahatmaji added, "Ahh,
now both eyes have opened up!"

****

Tonight we had just come from Varanasi, where we
spent a lot of time at the Kashi Vishwanath temple.
The first song the Mahatma played, before we talked
about going to the temple, was "Kashi Vishwanath
Gange," leaving us to wonder if we should mention it
or if He already knew all the details anyways!

Later, when we did mention it, He said, "That is why I
started with Kashi Vishwanath."

"Did you go to the Kumbha Mela?" Mahatmaji asked.

"No," we said, "we were loving Varanasi so much we
did not want to leave."

To let us know that we made the right decision,
Mahatmaji added with a smile, "The Kumbha Mela is
now Cell Phone Mela!" There was laughter from our
side, because there was an element of Truth in those
words.

****

"Sometimes, ideas come into my mind. Sixty years in
India, and sometimes a new thought comes. Today I
said something that I had never said before. This
morning I said it in a phone call, and this afternoon to
a tailor who sits by the roadside. That tailor is a very
noble man. He cannot read English or Hindi, but he
has knowledge of all the scriptures. I told him that
the television, the cell phone, the computers—now

you may not agree with me, but this is my conclusion—all of these are forms of Ravan.[64] All maya. They are the Ravan. Ravan had ten heads—it is symbolic. Meditate on this.

These characters are symbolic, the parts are acted out over and over again. This tailor does not read in English or Hindi, but how does he have a knowledge of everything? He understood and immediately agreed with what I said.

In Haradwar, the sadhus gather to eat, and they even chant some of Ravan's chants. You see, Ravan was very clever. In some parts of India they still worship him. Ravan was great in his austerity."

The Mahatma then sang us the melody of the chant, but claimed He had forgotten the words.

Interestingly, we had just been in Varanasi, where Sumakshi had purchased a CD with the "Ravan Stuti"—the very same chant that the Mahatma was humming. She took it as a gentle reminder to remember who wrote the chant.

He could protect us from things that we did not ask about, or even things that we did not know about! Such are the ways of one who is all One!

✳✳✳✳✳✳✳✳✳✳✳✳✳✳✳✳✳

There is no such thing as darkness, only varying degrees of light. (Quoted from Mahatmaji from *The Book of Mirdad*.)

✳✳✳✳✳✳✳✳✳✳✳✳✳✳✳✳✳

---

[64] Ravan is the demon king and villain that fights against Sri Ram in the Indian epic the *Ramayana*.

Often when visiting the Mahatma, we would stay at the ashram of Anandamayi Ma. Mahatmaji had many experiences with Ma, some of which are in *Transcendent Journey*. Here is a story that is not commonly known which He shared with us:

"The Raja of Solan once came to see Ma when She was staying with some devotees in a cave. The Raja asked Her, 'Who are you?' Often, to that question, She would answer, 'I am whoever you think I am.' But this time Ma gave a wonderful answer. She said, 'I am Dharshini.' She that gives darshan.

Whomever receives darshan from Ma for more than five minutes, even in a dream, Ma will be with them in the most trying part of their life. Who can make that promise?"

He added that there is a very good book about Ma called *Mother Reveals Herself*. Interestingly, the title of that book matches the subject of the story: Ma is Darshini.

The disciple of Ma in *Transcendent Journey* who was helped by Ma in the story of the car accident and the horoscope[65] was none other than the Indian architect for Chandigarh.[66]

There were two architects for Chandighar. There was a French architect (the Father) and an Indian (the

---

[65] Previously presented in this book.

[66] Chandigarh is the capital city of the Indian states of Punjab and Haryana in Northern India. It was the first planned city in India post-independence. Mahatmaji may have mentioned this because the French Architect is famous, and the Indian one virtually unknown, at least in history books.

Mother). The Indian was the Mother because he gave birth to the city.

✳✳✳✳✳✳✳✳✳✳✳✳✳✳✳✳

"In one of the scriptures, maybe the *Yoga Vashista*, I read of space travel. The bodies did not travel, only the mind—astral traveling.

In that scripture, they traveled far into space, and finally reached the center of darkness. But they continued moving through it, and eventually were moving at the speed of light, and perhaps even faster than the speed of light, and eventually they came out of the other side into another creation.

This dark area is Kali. Universes are created, and universes are destroyed by this darkness. Everything in creation comes from the Mother.

Even in Switzerland we have a temple to the Divine Mother. The black Madonna. Even the fierce aspects of Divine Mother can be seen in Switzerland.[67]

Kali and Mother are that black. That which gives birth to the universe and withdraws it again. Ramakrishna knew Kali that way, he had seen Her in meditation."

At that moment in the story, the lights went out for the satsang, never to return.

Very strange indeed, to be sitting with a Mahatma who is talking about the blackness of the Divine Mother of creation only to be plunged into darkness!

---

[67] He brought out a photo of the black Madonna surrounded by what in India are called Bhairavs, or fierce protectors.

The Mahatma just made light of it, saying that God must be listening, or maybe the government. "They heard me and they said, 'Enough!'"

✶✶✶✶✶✶✶✶✶✶✶✶✶✶✶✶✶

"Even in the dark you can have prasad. You can still find your mouth. You are not likely to put the food into your ear! There are two ears, and they produce dvaita. Two eyes for sight, and two nostrils for smell. But there is only one mouth. The mouth is advaitan![68]

To eat in Hindi means more than it does in English. You can eat insults, or criticisms. It is what you absorb."

✶✶✶✶✶✶✶✶✶✶✶✶✶✶✶✶✶

"It is written in every scripture, in every holy book, and yet human beings forget."

✶✶✶✶✶✶✶✶✶✶✶✶✶✶✶✶✶

The bible talks of two trees. The tree of life, which is the spinal system, and the tree of knowledge. Mankind was warned not to eat from the tree of knowledge. In Hindi, "to eat" means to absorb. We were not meant to commercialize knowledge, and when we do, it will mean the end of this planet. The ancients had great love for the Earth, and they protected Her.

✶✶✶✶✶✶✶✶✶✶✶✶✶✶✶✶✶

---

[68] Dvaita means "duality." Advaita, which is a whole school of yoga and philosophy, means "non-duality."

Sumakshi smelled gas in the kitchen and mentioned it to Jnananandaji.

"Oh really?" He replied, "I cannot smell at all. God took away my sense of smell."

"Has it always been that way?" Sumakshi asked.

"Oh no!" He replied, "I used to have a very acute sense of smell. God asks for the things that are the most..." and then He tapered off. "Anyway," He added, "He didn't have to ask."

****

"Ah... song birds have come."

****

Nowadays the Pope is having some problems, but the previous Pope, the one from Poland, he was an exceptional man. When he came to India, he got down onto his knees and he kissed the ground.

****

Tonight Mahatmaji told us a story He often told about His one power, "I have one power: I can help you remember everything or forget everything."

This time, instead of going into a long explanation, He simply said, "They all choose to forget."

Jnananandaji then turned to Sumakshi and asked if she remembered the story, and she replied that yes, indeed, she did.

"She remembers everything," Mahatmaji said with a grin, "and they forget everything!" He said pointing to the boys in the group (including me!).

"Lucky! They forget! She is a recorder."

This in itself was interesting, but then He added, "An artist must forget their art in order to sleep."

Often when Mahatmaji would tell this story, it was a joke, He would say, "You don't have to tell me right now, you can sleep on it!" (The joke being that when we sleep we forget everything in any case.)

Then, taking the whole thing a step further He said, "Humans like to forget. Then they come here to remember!"

****

When Jnananandaji was a young man, He loved to take photos of the Swiss alps with His "internal camera." Sharing the story with us one day, He said:

"In Zurich, I loved to take photos of mountains. Like this," and He blinked His eyes to illustrate. "I still take those photos," He said with a laugh. The eight kilometer walk that I take—I could take the entire walk without ever leaving this room." It was hard to believe, but by the knowing smile on His face you could see it was true.

He continued, "Some children had come to see me with their parents and I showed them how to take pictures with their eyes. They loved it! They took pictures of everything, especially of me. When they went back to Delhi, their friends asked them, 'Did you take pictures of Swamiji?'

The children answered, 'Yes!'

'Where are they?' the other children asked.

'In our heart,' the children replied."

"That is the thing," the Mahatmaji said, "One kind of picture you carry in the pocket, and the other you carry in your heart."

****

Jnananandaji knew a Bengali sweet-shop man. Describing him, Mahatma said, "Very intelligent. He always answers the phone saying 'Haan ji.' It is so much better than hello. Hello is hollow. Shallow! I told a government employee to start answering the phone saying 'haan ji.' It means 'yes' but it also implies 'I understand.' Many people started thinking he was the boss when they talked to him on the phone after that."

****

"Tomorrow I will sing you a song that I have in English. I will tell you a story about that song tomorrow. No... if I wait that long you will not be able to sleep," Mahatma directed His attention to one of the Brahmacharis and added, "so let me tell you now." And He sang the hymn "I Go Out in the Garden," but making a small change in the lyrics. He sang:

> I go out in the garden alone,
> While the dew is still on the roses,
> And the melody that You gave to me,
> The son of God discloses.

> And You walk with me,
> And You talk with me,
> And You tell me I am Your own.
> And the joy we share as we tarry there,
> None other has ever known.

In the original version of the song, the chorus is "and He walks with me, and He talks with me."

"Between the 'He' and the 'You,' it is just a little word, but it makes a big difference," Jnanananda said with a smile.

"Now I will tell you a story I have never told Steve before..."

Once there was a pundit in Vrindavan. You all have been to Vrindavan before? This man lived in a simple grass hut. Every morning he woke up and went to the temples and did his worship. His was a simple life.

One day, this pundit decided to go to Italy to see the Pope. So he arrived in Italy, and told them he was a pundit from India, and he managed to get a personal interview with the Pope.

When he went into the Pope's office, he saw a red telephone. He then asked the Pope, "What is that?"

"That is a direct line to God. It is only for emergencies. But when there is an emergency, you can call, and you can talk with God."

The pundit, of course, was amazed and asked if he could use it. The Pope thought for a minute, and then said, "Well, why not."

After about 10 minutes, the pundit hung up the phone. "That was amazing," he said, "now how much is the call?"

"Well," the Pope said, "God is a very long way away. It is a very long distance call. It is very expensive. About seventy-five Euros." The pundit was quite shocked, but he paid and off he went.

Years later, the Pope came to India and remembered the pundit from Vrindavan and decided to return the visit.

He searched around and finally found the grass hut, and inside was the pundit, and next to him was a red telephone.

"What is that for?" The Pope asked pointing to the red telephone.

"It is a direct line to God," the pundit answered.

"Do you think I could use it?" the Pope asked.

"Of course!" the pundit answered.

The Pope began to talk, and talked for a long time. He had many complaints: people don't come to church anymore, and this problem and that problem. After a long time, he hung up and turned to the pundit.

The Pope asked how much it would cost, but the pundit looked a little stunned.

"Nothing," the pundit said.

"Nothing at all?" now the Pope was shocked.

"No," the pundit said, "it is a local call."

✳✳✳✳✳✳✳✳✳✳✳✳✳✳✳✳✳

One day, Mahatmaji was handing out bananas for prasad and He said, "An apple a day…" With a gesture of His hand, He implied that He wanted us to finish the thought, and so someone replied, "Keeps the doctor away."

Then Mahatmaji said "A banana a day," and here there was a brief pause, "keeps the devil away!"

"Yes," He added, "keeps Shaitan away!"

He asked one of the Brahmacharis a question, but then, jokingly, added, "He needs another banana before he can answer! Shaitan! A long distance call!"

✳✳✳✳✳✳✳✳✳✳✳✳✳✳✳✳✳

Did I tell you the story of the scientist who could make energy out of the air? Jnananandaji looked at me with questioning eyes, and I did not know what to say, because He had told me, but I knew the others with me would love to hear the story. So I asked Him if He would not tell it for the benefit of others, and He consented.

A long time ago, in 1971, Jnananandaji was in Delhi visiting with a Mahatma who did not speak. He would use some sign language and then someone there would translate for him. On His way to visit this Mahatma, He ran into another Swami that He knew, just across the street.

At the house of the silent Mahatma, He met a young man, a scientist from Great Britain.

The young man asked Him if Jnananandaji knew of other mahatmas in the Delhi area. Jnanananda replied that He would not mention the names of other mahatmas in the house of a Mahatma. The young man was suitably impressed with the answer.

The next day, Jnananandaji saw the young man and then the day after that, and the very next day the silent Mahatma was on a train to the hills. On this day, Jnananandaji felt it was okay, and mentioned to the young Britisher that there was another Swamiji who Jnanananda knew who was just across the street.

The young British scientist was in hiding, actually. He had made a form of energy which had enough power to send a ship to the moon and back using only the power of the air.

This scientist was only 31 years old, but he had read many of the scriptures of India. "Yes it is all there," Mahatmaji said. "Everything is in everything. The Five elements. Yes, they are in everything. This man had discovered, in the driest area of earth, the sahara desert, how to produce water. All of the five elements are in everything. You see, Hanuman, his other name is Pavanputra, which means 'son of the wind.' The God of the wind carried Hanuman into his Mother's womb." Jnananandaji insinuated that Hanuman could fly using the power in air.

Later, this British scientist moved to Kerala to a cave and spent a year there practicing yoga and reading the scriptures. "I know that cave," Mahatmaji said.

He ended the story here today, but I believe that this is the very same scientist who later wrote a letter to the Mahatmaji saying, "Have failed in my attempt at yoga. Will return to science."

****

When tying a turban on His head, Mahatmaji made the comment that indeed a turban is difficult to tie without a mirror. Strangely, Bryan had been wearing a turban earlier in the day, and we all had been talking about that very subject.

Mahatmaji added that He had once given a talk about the dangers of mirrors. When the talk was over, a young girl, only five years old, approached the Mahatma to ask Him what was so dangerous. "You only look into the mirror," Mahatmaji replied, "when there is some trouble."

After a moment, He added, "Of course there are other reasons why you look into a mirror, but those I will not go into!" Everyone laughed.

"Do you know the story of Snow White? We all nodded yes. There is a mirror in that story as well— just see."

****

When the partition of India and Pakistan happened, they decided that the people in the mad house also had to be split.

A Mother brought her son to the mad house. You see, the doctors there can see how crazy someone is, the degree of craziness. So the Mother came and asked the doctor to have a look at her son.

Before the doctor could leave, the son stood up and said to the doctor, "You need to take a look at her," and he pointed to his Mother, "She is crazy!"

The doctor went down the hall to consult another doctor, and when he came back, he threw them both out, saying, "You don't belong here!"

During the partition though, the mad people had to be split into countries. I know because I knew a family that had a child in the mad house. He was extremely intelligent. He was living in Jalandhar.

When they moved some of them to India, the crazy people were saying, "We are not crazy, the people who divided the country are crazy!"

This young man who was so intelligent asked his brother to build a cage close to the road. Later, the young man lived there. He never left that cage. Whatever anyone fed him, he ate. He lived completely apart from the world.

****

Suddenly, Jnananandaji asked Bryan:

"What does the word 'religion' mean?"

Bryan replied, "I don't know."

"Is English your mother tongue?"

"Yes," Bryan replied. Then, after a pause, he said, "It means 'organized spirituality.'"

"Yes," Mahatmaji replied, and asked Bryan to repeat his definition. Then Mahatmaji said slowly,

"Organizing spirituality. This is what religion is doing. Religion means to return to one's origin. Antar Yantra.[69] It is the same word in Latin, Italian, French, English.

Most religions keep God at a safe distance."

****

"People ask me what is this place I stay in. I say it is a vridha ashram: an old people home. You are all very old, millions of years, and not just the few birthdays you have had here and there."

****

One day, someone asked the Mahatma about the Sri Yantra in the satsang room, and He was kind enough to comment:

"It is the first computer before computers. It is ancient and very powerful. I used to make them very often and paint them. I would make them just using a compass. Four triangles going upward intersect with four going down—Shiva and Shakti. It also is the sahasrara."[70]

In addition to those characteristics, the Mahatma said that the yantra contains each of the 43 Sanskrit characters—the same as the thousand-petaled lotus.

The Sri Yantra has great power, but the Mahatma also mentioned that if the power is not used properly then it will be reversed. It can really be a weapon.

---

[69] Antar Yantra means "the inward journey."

[70] Sahasrara is the Sanskrit name for the thousand-petaled lotus, or the crown chakra at the top of the head.

There were people that built a machine that measures the energy of anything. Whatever you put in front of it, it will tell you the energy. When a Sri Yantra was put in front of the machine, it fell over.

✸✸✸✸✸✸✸✸✸✸✸✸✸✸✸✸✸

The Mahatmaji's Mother moved in very high circles in Europe. One day, Mahatmaji told us that she knew the psychologist Carl Jung, as well as Herman Hesse and many great minds of that time.

When Jnananandaji went to India, His Mother went to Jung and told him that her son was moving to India to become a sadhu. Jung knew the teachings of India, and yet he said to her that He was moving to be with mad people. A man is recognized by his companions.[71] (That saying comes from India, actually.) Jung would not say that the young man was crazy, but that was implied.

Maharaj's Mother was quite smart in her own way. She wanted the Mahatma to be a banker, yet she told Him never to borrow money from people and never to lend it to them. To give people money was okay, but do not lend it.

The Mahatma then noted that Switzerland eventually got into trouble with the banks.

When the Mahatma was a young man, He knew a man named Rosenzweig, meaning "branch of a rose." In that time, it was the custom for many Jews to adopt names that were easier to pronounce for Westerners, and such was the case with Rosenzweig.

---

[71] "Jaisa Sangh, vaisa rang," I believe is the saying.

"He taught me chess," Mahatmaji said, "so that I could play in chess league even while I was only fifteen. He told me in 1941, when I was twelve, that Hitler will lose. At this time Hitler was winning everything. I asked why he thought that and he replied 'Economy. Hitler has no back-up economy.'"

The young Jnanananda asked if there was anything that can get Switzerland into trouble. Rosenzweig replied, "Its banking system that allows corrupt people, thieves, mafia, and criminals to store their money."

"Mind you, this was in 1941, and now, seventy years later, this is a big problem. The Swiss government has to answer questions."

✷✷✷✷✷✷✷✷✷✷✷✷✷✷✷✷

"For years I have bought only two things from the chemist shop around the corner,"Jnananandaji said. "I buy Vitamin C, which protects you from the cold, and I buy Vitamin E, which is good for the skin."

After many years of this, one day the chemists asked Him, "How is it possible that you only take these two kinds of medicine?"

"All I need is the three vitamins," the Mahatma responded.

The two chemists at the store looked at one another, and then looked at Him questioningly.

"Yes," He said, "Vitamin C, Vitamin E, and Vitamin M."

Again they looked at one another, because they had not heard of Vitamin M. Looking questioningly at Mahatmaji they received the answer that it is "something that sadhus use."

"Oh," the man from the shop replied, "you mean meditation?"

The Mahatma laughed and laughed. "No," He said, "something else."

The truth was that sadhus were not meant to use the word "money." Sripad Baba used to refer to it as papers, and I believe it was Nirvedananda from Vashista Guha who referred to it as Vitamin M.

****

"Do you know the secret of the sandhya?[72] Steve, do you remember?"

"Yes, sir," I replied.

"Then tell them."

"Sir, at the sandhya, every day, all beings, animals and humans, leave their body for a moment and touch into the Spirit."

"Yes," Mahatmaji replied, "I once knew a kriya yogi who had a place in Mussoorie, where I had my kutir. He was not my disciple, no, but he shared with me his experience. At times he would be driving the car and he would leave the body. Then he would come to his garage in Kolkata, and then he would return to the

---

[72] Sandyha is the twilight hour.

body. This may seem very far-fetched, but the truth is, I know this also from my own experience."

Mahatmaji added that even scientifically there are more accidents at the twilight hour.

****

When talking about the ruin with the amazing acoustics one day, Jnananandaji said, "I can feel the spirit of those that were in that place long ago."

Vinod was interested. "How can you see?" he asked.

"There are ghosts," Mahatmaji replied.

"How do you know?" Vinod asked.

Maharaj said, "Bhoot ko bhoot hi pehchanta hai." (Which translates to, "It takes a ghost to see a ghost.")

A sadhu can recognize a sadhu, a thief a thief, a doctor a doctor, etc.

****

On this night, seemingly by accident, Jnananandaji taught me one of the most beautiful and most simple lessons He had ever taught.

A devotee came into the satsang while the Mahatma was engrossed in telling a story. The story was about complete concentration. When trying to commune with nature, for example, you should not bring a cell phone or any other form of distraction.

The man prostrated himself, and then quietly went to the back of the room without receiving the biscuit that was a customary gesture of welcome from the saint.

A little bit later, Maharaj noticed him and asked, "Did he come here?" Then in Hindi He added, "He did not get his biscuit?"

"No, Swamiji," the disciple responded, "I came there but you didn't notice."

"Ahhhhh," the Mahatma said thoughtfully, "my mind was one tracked. I was focused on something else. Why didn't you say something?"

"Swamiji," the devotee replied, "I did not want to disturb you."

"Dis-turb", the Mahatmaji uttered the word as though it was something that He was trying to remember that had long been forgotten. Then, more comically, He said, "Dees-THURB" as though the word itself was completely comical.

"We would not have this life if we did not want to be disturbed."

Sumakshi was laughing with her mouth open and Mahatmaji was quick to add, "Ha! She has not been able to close her mouth. It has affected her."

This, like so many of the Mahatmaji's stories, works on many levels. A simple one, though, is that even in seva I sometimes would be counting time. Feeling this person is disrupting me, and I have something to do. But who is it that is doing the disrupting? It is God. Everything comes from the hand of the Guru. How can helping someone or sharing with someone be a distraction? If the Guru treated us that way, we would never move forward, even an inch.

It was a great lesson, in a simple package, from a great friend.

✶✶✶✶✶✶✶✶✶✶✶✶✶✶✶✶✶

Mahatmaji said one day in satsang, "Conversation is copper, singing is silver, and silence is golden."

"Wah!"[73] He exclaimed, "Here is something original that came out. I have not said that in sixty years! It is something new."

The thrill of the moment reminded me of the time He clapped for himself after remembering a complex song in English. As He finished the song, He nearly jumped out of His seat and quickly walked across the room clapping and saying, "Oh. Wah! Wah!"

What was so thrilling to see, was that this action had not even the slightest hint of ego in it. You could see He was so delighted to see what Divine Mother had done. He was just like a child full of joy and enthusiasm.

After we all thought about it for a moment, He glanced at one of the Brahmacharis. "Do you believe this?" He asked in a voice of mock seriousness.

Before the Brahmachari could answer, He added, "One eye is closed—perhaps you believe only halfway?"

---

[73] "Wah" roughly translates to "wow" or "fantastic."

After a moment, the Brahmachari said, "Sir, some kinds of conversation seem less than copper."

"Yes," the Mahatma said. Then, with a burst of energy, He replied, "Yes—it's plastic!" That, of course, resulted in a room full of laughter.

Then, after a short silence, He added that of course there were some types of conversation that were plastic. The kind, for example, that you read in the newspaper.

After a laugh, He guided things back to harmony. "No, let it be copper," He said, "a pure metal. It is not soooo bad also." Being in the company of the Mahatma, and hearing His wonderful stories, we all had to agree!

✱✱✱✱✱✱✱✱✱✱✱✱✱✱✱✱

Talking about copper, silver, and gold, got the Mahatma talking about Vitamin M.

"You know money used to be copper, silver, and gold. The coins today…" Mahatmaji laughed and let the sentence taper off.

"I know a man from Belgium, a writer, who says that money will not last."

On a more serious note, He added, "Diseases travel with it—the coins and the paper money. One should ALWAYS wash their hands after handling money. That is why money will not last."

✱✱✱✱✱✱✱✱✱✱✱✱✱✱✱✱

Talking about newspapers and how the Mahatma used to call the newspaper the vairagya patr, He told this story:

Once, when the newspaper man came, Jnananandaji asked the boy to go and get Him a vairagya patr. The boy went to the newspaper man outside, and told him he wanted a vairagya patr.

"Hmmmmm," the newspaper man was thinking. "Would that be Times of India or the Metro Paper?"

Later on, Maharaj started to call the paper the pagal patr—meaning "the paper that leads one to insanity"!

Strangely, for years He had been telling this story, but tonight He added a wonderful tale from His own youth:

When Maharaj was a young man, He was very curious, and so He once went to the mad house, and He asked the man in charge to take Him to see the craziest person.

When He got to that man, Maharaj asked him, "What made you crazy?" And the man replied, "Reading the newspaper."

Maharaj then said, "Everyone in the world is crazy. Even those in this room are crazy... except perhaps for Steve and I."

Laughter filled the room of course.

✶✶✶✶✶✶✶✶✶✶✶✶✶✶✶✶

Talking about tree therapy one day, the Mahatma added some interesting thoughts about nature and mankind:

"Some pilgrims from France came here and one lady asked 'What is the difference between a tree and a human?'"

"Without hesitating a moment, I replied that the tree wants to talk to the human, but the human does not want to talk to the tree. It is true. We only want to talk to the tree when we need something."

Mimicking the average person, He said, "I am taking this fruit. I will cut you!"

"The tree hears all this," the Mahatma stated plainly. "It understands. A healthy tree is alive."

"We must learn how to talk to it, but when you do, there must be total concentration. No cell phones. No restlessness. Absolute focus."

"When I go on my walk, there are three very old trees. I take them mithai,[74] I offer them Gangajal. Not every time," He added, "but sometimes."

"I embrace them."

The saint had a big enough heart for all of us, and for every living being on this planet.

✶✶✶✶✶✶✶✶✶✶✶✶✶✶✶✶

Paramhansa Yogananda had once told Paramananda about three of his past lives. Paramananda later met a

---

[74] Mithai is a term for Indian sweets.

Frenchman who told him that this was of no use. "Ask him," the Frenchman said, "to SHOW you your lives."

Talking about people who visit him, Maharaj said, "Many people come and say, 'We were together these three past lives.'"

Then the Mahatma added, "We have all been together."

"Sometimes one recognizes a place or a person from his eyes. That is a memory of a past life."

Smiling at us, Mahatmaji added, "But you are not YET fully awake."

These were words to meditate on: "fully awake," when all time spirals around the center in the Eternal Now.

****

Today at Mahatmaji's was a day of great silence, a more silent satsang than usual.

At the door of Mahatmaji's camp, He greeted us with a story. Jyoti (the Mother of Mukunda, who is a very special child whose tale is in *Transcendent Journey*) had called.

"I asked her," He said, "if she had found a medicine for laughter."

Of course we all laughed, and Mahatmaji replied, "Oh, more laughter! But today will be a more serious satsang."

After some stories, we all fell into a silent mood, absorbed, listening, and just being in the company of the saint.

After some time, He said, "The sound... of silence."

"You must be able to hear the sound of this house."

"Vedanta begins with shravana.[75] It is the first thing."

Then, from the silence, He asked a Brahmachari, "Who is the Guru in your ashram?"

"Yogananda... Kriyananda," the Brahmachari replied.

"But the Indian tradition is that the Guru must be living," Mahatmaji stated plainly. "You could have met him in person—before he leaves the body. Do you have a Guru mantra?"

When no reply came, Maharaj further shared about the Guru mantra: "When you are in meditation, of course you hear Om, but within Om is a specific mantra. In kriya, you can hear many things. The atoms of the universe."

"These are after-effects of kriya. You can hear the mantra. You can even see the mantra. Isn't it fascinating?! You see the mantra. That is why they are called seers."

"One woman came here and she got initiation from Yogananda in a dream. It can happen like that also, but the Guru initiates you. There must be some contact."

---

[75] Shravana means listening.

"But you are all doing the right thing. You are on the right track."

"Kriyananda," the Mahatmaji said after a pause, "Who would name someone that? He was not named by an Indian. It is like 'Karmananda.' Well, that is okay. Kriya means many things. The last rites—kriyas—they talk about iccha shakti, kriya shakti, and gyan shakti. First desires, then the purification. (Kriya is purification. It is a very important stage.) And then you reach."

When I came to the Mahatma as a young Brahmachari, He said the same thing to me, and I could not help but think that this was for the benefit of the young Brahmacharis who accompanied me on that day.

Satsang room

****

On this more silent satsang, Jnananandaji spoke about the dangers of too much thinking.

"Don't think too much. It will lead to illness."

"The mind goes on," He gestured in a way like someone was talking way too much. "Use the heart."

"Ravan had ten heads. One is quite enough! I say, as long as you have a head, you have a headache!

I tell everyone to wear pagrees[76] to prevent headaches. The women in some areas in India wear turbans—to keep their minds from wandering.

Tie the head up, then you will be less likely to have a headache."

Then, when the silence descended again, He said "So many things to say, so many things to be silent about."

****

The Mahatma one day told us about a transport minister who had a near-death experience.

"I met him only for a little while. Someone took me over to see him because he was dying of some disease. Then, some days later, his wife phoned me that something strange has happened, please come over. I went. She told me that a few days ago, Ajit had symptoms as if he was dead. Naturally, the wife and daughters started weeping.

He was, in fact, out of his body and near the ceiling in one corner of the room watching his body and them.

---

[76] A pagree is a turban.

When he re-entered the body, he told them 'Please! Do not weep when I die. Nothing happens to me, only my body is gone.' It is amazing that people are given these experiences while living."

✸✸✸✸✸✸✸✸✸✸✸✸✸✸✸✸

Once, a group of us were talking, and a Brahmachari mentioned to Mahatmaji that his parents were divorced.

Mahatmaji became somewhat serious for a moment and then said, "Yes, nowadays this has become a fashion in the West and even over here. Divorce, as recently as my childhood, was unheard of."

"I once heard of an American couple divorcing because she did not clean the table properly. Absurd. It is a true story."

"In earlier times, people used to understand that the wife represents all women, and the man all husbands. Now there is misunderstanding and intolerance of each other."

"Earlier, they realized that once they were married, it was a commitment until death."

✸✸✸✸✸✸✸✸✸✸✸✸✸✸✸✸

One day we brought a Shiva lingam, which we had attained in Varanasi, for the Mahatma to bless. We brought it in a copper vessel and used stones to help it stand straight. Commenting on this, He said:

"Your lingam is very interesting. Instead of these stones, when you put it properly, use shaligram fossils. That works well with Shiva lingams. You can still get them in Haradwar."

The Mahatma then took from His own altar a few shaligram fossils of shells, that looked something like spiral pasta or curled caterpillars, to show us.

"Badrinarayan's statue is also shaligram, it is not man-made."

He then showed us the picture He had of Badrinarayan, from a rare book written by Yogananda's younger brother's son-in-law who took the picture in 1946.

As a final point on the topic, Mahatmaji said, "Dharma is buried under a shaligram."

✷✷✷✷✷✷✷✷✷✷✷✷✷✷✷✷✷

One day later in our visit, the Mahatma spoke again on the subject of shaligrams. Shaligrams are small black rocks that come from Mukteshwar in Nepal. The first book that Jnananandaji read on India, was by an American who wrote it in Mukteshwar. It is an ancient place.

The Mahatma recommended that the lingam be kept up with shaligram fossils, and recommended a wooden yoni. "It must always be placed in the Mother. It connects it to the earth. It connects it back to that dark center, the black hole, the darkness behind it."

He mentioned that, while traveling, the lingam does not need to be in the base.

He also showed us a picture of the black Madonna and the dark aspect of Divine Mother in various bhavs, and spoke a little about the frightening aspects of Divine Mother, called Bhairavs.

★★★★★★★★★★★★★★★★★

One day in satsang, observing someone laughing, the Mahatma remarked, "He is a good actor."

"All human beings are actors. Actors on the stage of death. Life. I have written it in a poem. I tell people to read 'The Book of Life.' It is very important. There are four stages. Dreaming, waking, deep sleep, and then the state of the soul, turiya."

"Even in deep sleep you are conscious, because you can say 'I slept well. I slept happily.' By reading the book of this life, the last stage, the soul state, can be," the Mahatma then repeated for emphasis, "CAN be revealed. But the attitude with which you read this book is very important."

★★★★★★★★★★★★★★★★★

One day in satsang, Jnananandaji mentioned that in 1980 He had been to Shirdi and witnessed a miracle. "I had been unwell for a month, with a cough and cold. I got a room to rest in, and ate some ash from the dhoni of Shirdi,[77] and locked myself in the room for a day. The next day I was fine. I had recovered completely."

★★★★★★★★★★★★★★★★★

---

[77] A dhoni is a sacred fire that is usually kept continuously burning. Shirdi is where Sai Baba lived.

Mahatmaji lovingly spoke about one of the disciples, saying, "He is a blissful man. He never falls sick."

✶✶✶✶✶✶✶✶✶✶✶✶✶✶✶✶

One day before we reached Mahatmaji's camp, Sumakshi had had a slightly difficult moment. When we walked in, Jnananandaji did not recognize her. He said, "Who is this?"

"Oh!" He exclaimed, recognizing her, "Sometimes birds change their feathers."

During that same satsang, the Mahatma asked someone about going to Italy.

"Will you fly?" the Mahatma asked, placing great emphasis on the word "fly" and flapping His hands like wings in an aeronautically ephemeral gesture!

"You were all birds in a previous incarnation," the Mahatma said with a big, enthusiastic smile.

"Yes," He added, "Flying... Flying!"

✶✶✶✶✶✶✶✶✶✶✶✶✶✶✶✶

Once, Sumakshi arrived early and found Sri Jnananandaji waiting by the gate for us, and so the two waited outside for myself and the others to arrive.

Two older men walked by, and the Mahatma said, "I see them every day, walking so sweetly together. It is so interesting, watching people going by and seeing what is in all their minds. Hah!" He clapped His hands gleefully. "Very interesting, but you don't take it too seriously! Just watch and enjoy!"

When we went inside, we noticed that He had placed the Shiva lingam that we had brought from Varanasi on a stand on another inverted bowl. "The Shiva lingam has become higher," He said, "it has grown."

****

Jnananandaji and Sumakshi were in the kitchen one day, when the Mahatma said to her, "Do you know that there is a woman on the internet who is teaching people how to live without eating? Have you heard of such a thing?"

"Yes, Swamiji," Sumakshi replied, "I think Steve met her. She is Australian and spends time in Thailand."

"Aaa!" He exclaimed with great enthusiasm, "How do you know?! She knows everything! How does she know?"

Overhearing the conversation, Bryan and I started laughing, and the Mahatma said, "Steve is laughing!"

"It's because he knows I do not know everything, Swamiji!" Sumakshi replied.

"Steve!" He yelled loudly from the kitchen, "She knows everything!"

"It's true, Swamiji!" I replied.

The Mahatma then pulled out a paper and saw that the name of the woman who could live without food was Yasmuheen. He then looked straight at Bryan, who had been having some issues with food, and asked "Would you like to know how to live without food or water?"

"Yes, I think I would," he replied.

"Hmmm. Let me tell you a story."

The Mahatma then told us the tale of the five rishis and Brahma.

"You see, the five wisest rishis went to Brahma and told Him that the world would be better without the stomach and this feeling of hunger. Brahma thought over this, and said He was willing to try it, but it was not likely to turn out well.

Nevertheless, Brahma agreed to do an experiment for 40 days. No food was grown. No food was cooked. People had nothing to do. They became politicians and gamblers and got into all kinds of mischief! At one point, the rishis had to come back to Brahma and beg him to return the world to its previous condition. The stomach at least helps to keep it somewhat in control."

The Mahatma went on to mention that Paramahansa Yogananda knew two people who did not eat. One in Germany and one in Bengal.

The main saint of Switzerland did not eat or drink. He had ten children. He left his home when the youngest was only 2 months old. (He took permission from the mother of the children first.) "Some of his descendants," the Mahatma continued, "came here to Rishikesh."

The woman is nine years older than her husband. She came with her daughters, who could see the auras of everything, including trees. "It is a gift," He said, "probably it has come down through the family."

"Yogananda said of Indians going to America that the environment can be stronger than the will power. It can pull you, and he also felt it. He went to the U.S.A. with twelve lessons. Once he arrived there, people laughed and said, 'more than this is needed, it has to be made clearer.'"

Speaking of His own teacher, Mahatmaji said, "My Guru had no use for those lessons, because a lot of these things were already known in India, but once I was put in charge of the lessons. I asked my Guru that here it talks of first kriya, then the second, the third, and finally the fourth."

"Why don't you give higher kriyas?" the young disciple asked.

Atmananandaji laughed and said, "Those higher kriyas are only for those that haven't been able to do the first one properly, and need some more entertainment. More things to do!"

✶✶✶✶✶✶✶✶✶✶✶✶✶✶✶✶✶

There was once a Sufi saint who lived with his dog. He was a simple and happy saint. One day, he heard that they were gathering all the dogs together in one place. They were not going to hurt the dogs, but they wanted to get rid of them, so they were putting them all in a temple. (The actual word He used was a Hindi word, sheesh mahal, which literally translates to "palace of mirrors.")

This was not, however, a palace of normal mirrors. You know those mirrors—they have them in every country. Some make you look thin and others make you look tall. They were taking all of the dogs and putting them in this building full of mirrors that distort your reflection.

Once in the palace of mirrors, the dogs were given food and water and everything they would need, but when the dogs would see the other dogs in the mirror, they would start barking and barking. Soon, those dogs died.

Now, in all of the country there was only one dog left, the dog that belonged to the saint. So the government came to the saint and asked to take the dog.

"Of course," the saint said, "feel free to take him."

When the dog got to the building, though, he was put into the palace of mirrors, but he did not bark. He lived with a saint after all, and so he was calm. He was there one day, and then two days, three days, and not a single bark, and so he did not die. He just ate the food they gave him and got fatter!

Finally, the authorities took that dog back to the saint. They could not help but ask about it. It was a miracle. This dog never barked or growled.

The saint just smiled and said, "He knows that there is no other." (He actually said in Hindi, "Yeh janta hai ki dusra to koi hai hi nahi!")

Later, about the same story, Mahatmaji commented: there is a deep teaching in this.

✳✳✳✳✳✳✳✳✳✳✳✳✳✳✳✳

When going on His walk, there was a house that used to attract the Mahatmaji. It was in a quiet place, and was a beautiful house, very origin-al, and full of flowers.

When passing by, Mahatmaji used to take a photo with His eyes and pause for a moment. Sometimes He would see an older couple out on the veranda.

Then, one day during that pause, they saw the Mahatma and invited Him in. The man was a teacher of mathematics. It turns out that he had been the teacher of Maitreyi's husband, and also of her sister, and the two grandchildren of the man where Jnananandaji lived in Mussourie for so many years. Some of Jnananandaji's other disciples had been his students, so they knew many people in common. "There was a kind of familiarity," He said, "as if we had known each other a long time."

"I told them that this house was origin-al! Most houses are copies. There is a house industry."

The day He told this story, the Mahatmaji had seen them after they had been away for eight months. "I go on that walk perhaps five times a week," He said, "and I always pause at that house."

When He saw them, He told them, "Yes, I have seen you here many times during my walk in the last eight months."

During that time, they were in Bangalore. But perhaps their minds were in the house, or perhaps the house was so origin-al that it expressed something of their essence, and the Mahatmaji would pause just to appreciate that.

Later, He commented that a Finnish artist had designed His kutir in Mussoorie. "I have always lived in origin-al places. I am lucky."

****

The Mahatma sang an amazing version of the chant "I Am Om" today. It was so amazing, it seemed to surprise even the Mahatma himself, who said, "Wah! Very powerful! If we keep singing like this, we will not know where we are!"

Indeed, we all felt transported in His bliss.

****

One night, Jnananandaji told us enchanting stories of Kalinjar, which truly sounded like a magical place. Kalinjar is located in the Bundelkhand region of central India, between Panna and Chitrakoot. Traveling with another man, the two of them arrived in the area at night, excited to immediately explore.

The local people advised against going around at nighttime. Wild animals roamed there, and it was dangerous.

Undeterred, the two men managed to find a torch, and when the townspeople saw that they were serious, one of them stepped forward and offered to guide them.

In this mystical place, you passed through five kilometers, and there were five boundary walls. Near the fourth boundary wall, there was a lake. After the fifth boundary wall, they came upon a plateau, and on that plateau were thousands of murtis.[78] Heads, horses, and every kind of murti you can imagine.

A few kilometers from there was a place called Sita Kund.[79] Sita Kund had in it the bed where Sitaji used to sleep. A very ornate and very origin-al piece.

"There was a man who was staying there. Not a Swami exactly—actually he was a tantric. He could touch you and then tell you the Guru mantra. Yes, he took my pulse and then told me the Guru mantra. He took the pulse of the man I was with and said, 'Main karoon?' (The man was repeating, 'What should I do?') That is what he was thinking."

The tantric had another trick to tell the future. He would place four rocks and then ask you to touch one. As Jnananandaji touched one, the man shared with Him some helpful words about His future.

The well that Sitaji had used for water was still in that place, although by the time the Mahatma was there it was in a broken condition, mostly mud and dirt with just a tiny bit of water. The tantric was cleaning out this well, so that it could be used again as a seva to the Gods.

Six months, or perhaps a year later, Swamiji returned to that place, but the tantric was dead. He had finished his work though. Pure, clean water once again flowed from the well.

✶✶✶✶✶✶✶✶✶✶✶✶✶✶✶✶

---

[78] A murti is a statue.

[79] Sita, of course, is the wife of Sri Ram, of the Ramayana, and much adored in India. A kund is a pool or a well.

I think it was on that same journey where Mahatmaji met a caretaker who asked if he could cook dinner for the Mahatma and His friend. They agreed, and, after the meal, the caretaker asked to massage the Mahatma's feet.

"Now, my Guru could not go to sleep without someone doing this seva," the Mahatma said, "but I had never really let anyone massage my feet."

Someone said, "Prepare for the surprise of your life if you let this happen."

"So, hesitatingly, I put my foot out; my companion also looked suspiciously on. Then, this man began pressing my toes and suddenly such a wave of relaxation came over my whole body, it was amazing! I asked him what he was doing and he explained that there were seventy-two thousand nerves in the body, maybe five or seven major ones in the legs, and he knew how to stimulate them. I asked him to show me a nerve in my leg and, without looking, he just put his hand under my knee and pressed and I felt an electric current go from my foot all the way up my spine to my head! He had a Guru who had taught him this and he would also pass this knowledge on to a qualified disciple. But it was not to be commercialized. They could earn their living doing other things, but this knowledge was to be kept pure."

"This was a science," the Mahatma added, "from ancient India."

✶✶✶✶✶✶✶✶✶✶✶✶✶✶✶✶✶

Jnananandaji was once eating a dessert with a man who was saying how much he was enjoying that dessert. Yes. It had a wonderful taste.

Then Jnananandaji asked, "Is it that the dessert has a wonderful taste, or is that taste coming from your mouth?"

It seemed like a simple sort of question, and the man took another bite of his food and then stopped to ponder. "I don't know. Give me a day to think about it," the man said.

But the man could not stop thinking, and that night he lay in bed awake pondering the issue.

The next day the man came to the Mahatma's house and said, "What is the answer? Please tell me. I have not been able to sleep all night!"

"Now," Mahatmaji said, "I will tell you something that I told to the tailor on my walk, and he very much grasped the meaning: I have cut the fabric three times, and it is still too short."[80]

Bryan gave a good laugh. "See!" Mahahatmaji said with a smile.

"This refers to the lifestyle of the people. Of course it can refer to other things as well—to your job or even to your spiritual practices. Yes. All kinds of different things.

I could easily tell you the answer, but this one I will leave for you as homework. Don't take it too seriously though. It is not worth losing sleep over."

✷✷✷✷✷✷✷✷✷✷✷✷✷✷✷✷✷

---

[80] In Hindi, "Teen bar kata, phir bhi chota."

On a different occasion, Maharaj told the above story and ended by saying, "See, everything is inside you!"

****

Jnananandaji one night mentioned His favorite Devata, but I did not catch the name. That Devata had seen the advent of Ram 20 times, and had seen the advent of Krishna 15 times.

"These things all go in cycles," was the Mahatma's simple reply.

****

One night, one of the disciples came in to kneel at Jnananandaji's feet, and, as usual, the Mahatma handed the man some biscuits. The man said there was egg in the biscuits, and refused to take them.

"Why do you think they have egg?"

"The color, Swamiji."

"Ahhh…. you see he is clairvoyant."

I must have looked a little surprised or questioning, because the Mahatma added, "He can see that which is not visible."

The Mahatma did not usually take egg, but He added then that if it was "invisible" (meaning in a cake or a cookie), it did not bother him.

Later in the satsang, Mahatmaji mentioned clairvoyants again while telling us about His cave in Mussoorie.

In Mussoorie there is a cave, it is about the size of the room where we had the satsangs. "We used to do kirtan there with a sitar player, and, in fact, some of the first cassette recordings were done in that very cave."

Once, a clairvoyant came there and said that Aurangzeb's treasure was buried there—either that or there was a great yogi in samadhi meditating there. Those were the vibrations in that place.

Strange, in the two stories, He never gives a lot of credence to clairvoyants. That said, the day before, He had given a satsang where He talked about the Guru mantra, and said that first you need to find the mantra within the Om vibration. After that, you eventually see the mantra inside of yourself. That is why they used to be called "seers," but those things have lost their true meaning these days.

****

Today, a few people from our group were departing. The Mahatma's simple and wonderful comment:

"Trains are thieves. They take people away!"

Commenting on the power of the satsang He said:

"After coming here, no one goes back, they only go forward."

****

One day we brought Maharaj flowers—yellow lilies, red roses and a twig of bougainvillea. The Mahatma asked Sumakshi to arrange them. As she was about to take them He noticed the roses and asked, "Are those roses? You better put them separately in another vase. Roses don't like to be in competition with other flowers."

****

Sensing a certain something in the air at satsang, Jnananandaji said, "Something is brewing today." And He pointed at the brain.

"Chai?" Sumakshi said with a smile.

"Yes!" the Mahatma replied with a large smile, "Chai!"

****

"In the forest where I walk, there is a rock," the Mahatma explained, "and when I look at it from a certain angle, I can see two eyes. I feel someone is in there."

The Mahatma paused for a moment and we all must have looked a little surprised.

"Oh! Yes!" He exclaimed with the excitement of a child, "It can happen. I sometimes take some flowers and gangajal and mithai to that rock, as I did today. I usually sit nearby and rest for a few minutes. It is known to happen. You have heard of Ahalya? In the Ramayana she was turned to stone and came to life only when Rama touched her."[81]

All of us were surprised to hear this tale from a saint, but later when we went on that walk, Sumakshi found that very same rock, although it was hard to make out the eyes exactly.

---

[81] Ahalya cheated on her husband Rishi Gautama with Indra, the king of the Gods. As punishment, Rishi Gautama turned Ahalya into stone.

The next day, Mahatmaji came into the kitchen while Sumakshi was there and said, "Today you are going to learn some secret things. Oh yes! Secrets that you never knew."

Sumakshi told the Mahatma that we had found the rock on our walk. The rock even had some flowers and some sweets on it.

"You FOUND it!!" He exclaimed. "That is amazing! Only an artist can find it!" He then told us the proper angle to look from to see the face. He had been there this afternoon eating mithai and then left some on the rock as an offering.

Sumakshi wrote in her journal: "I had felt so touched on seeing it. How much compassion this man had. That poor soul inside the rock must be thirsty for love and no one knew it was there. What a punishment. And then finally someone comes along, realizes it is in there, and shares with it sweets and flowers even though it is in a form that will not incite love from most beings. It is heartbreakingly sweet and inspiring."

Where else can you find a being whose love and compassion extends into every facet of life, even into realms that most of us cannot see?

✱✱✱✱✱✱✱✱✱✱✱✱✱✱✱✱✱

Talking one day about the garden of some friends, He said, "The flowers in the garden of that South Indian couple are sooo beautiful. You almost feel like they are trying to speak to you. It can be done. Earlier there was only one language. Man has forgotten it, but animals know it, trees know it. You can speak to them and they will talk back. Even 'the rock' knows this language."

✳✳✳✳✳✳✳✳✳✳✳✳✳✳✳✳✳

One day in a satsang with several foreigners, the Mahatma admitted that He had a mantra that could produce instant wealth. The problem was, that those foreigners were already well-off financially, and they did not really need the help, and so He did not tell them. As He was telling us about it, He said, "This mantra is only for the poor. And you all are living this life, so I think you are not wealthy."

In a kind of hushed tone so that others might not hear He said, "I can tell you the mantra. It is...never... count... your... money." For emphasis, He let that thought hang in the air for a moment, then began again, "You can count money you are responsible for, when you are making payments and that sort of thing, but NEVER count it to see how much you have. A beggar with a few rupees will feel he needs more, a person with a few thousand needs more thousands. A person with lakhs needs more lakhs. It is psychology! Never count it."

That very day, Sumakshi had been telling me that she was worried about spending 700 dollars on a plane ticket to Italy. She just recently was trying to figure out how much money she had to help decide about the ticket. The Mahatma never missed even a single thought that might be of help.

✳✳✳✳✳✳✳✳✳✳✳✳✳✳✳✳✳

In His abode, Maharaj had a small Gita Yantra made by Krishnanath Sharma. It contained the entire text of the *Bhagavad Gita* written in tiny letters into a kind of circular mandala surrounding an image of Sri Krishna. The yantra was given by the Rani of Rajinder Nagar. (The Rani used to refer to the Mahatma as her second son.)

Interestingly, this Gita Yantra was written in an anticlockwise direction. Krishnanath's sons also made these now, only five times larger. One of the brothers was Vishwananth Sharma, who happened to live in Mussoorie.

Once, the Mahatma was traveling with Vishwanath, as well as Janaki and another lady. The lady said she had never seen any miracles in India, but only had met Babas. The Mahatma said, "Now you have asked for it!"

The group met a man who wrote some things on a piece of paper, and then gave a piece of paper to the lady. He asked her to write five cities, five countries, five vegetables... a total of 25 things. Then he asked her for her paper. He opened his and he had written exactly the same things!

The man asked which perfume of what kind of flower they would like to smell. One answered rose, and the scent of rose was, indeed, there. Another answered jasmine, and the distinct scent of jasmine emanated from his palm.

Later, that man invited the Mahatma and His group for a meal. They were opposite Whitefield in Dehradun, and the man asked Jnanananda what fruits were growing in the orchard there. The Maharaj named them, all that He could remember, but was informed by the man that one had been forgotten. In answer to the question of which one, the man pulled a newspaper from his lap and there were 10 green chestnuts.

That man then proceeded to call on a spirit named Salim, by picking up a stick and holding it to his ear like a phone. Upon being told that Salim was busy, he called Hazrat. After the spirit was summoned, the man said that it would take five minutes, because Hazrat was coming from New York! At that point a yellow butterfly or moth came in. The Mahatma admitted, "We were all a bit scared as it circled around our heads and finally settled on the man's shoulder."

The man said that in 33 days he could teach the art of controlling a spirit, a ghost.

In a later satsang, Maitreyi told us that this man eventually wound up in jail.

The Rani of Rajinder Nagar's husband died on Janmashtami. Instead of mourning, she celebrated Krishna leelas everywhere. The Mahatma had celebrated many a Janmashtami enacting the Leela of Krishna and Radha by dressing up children. Mahatmaji added with a smile, "Next time, you can be Krishna," He said, nodding at me, "and Sumakshi can be Radha." Noticing a young Brahmachari who was there with us He said, "You can be the cowherd."

I felt in this little story a kind of invitation to see Sumakshi as Radha, and try and treat her with that kind of deep, reverential, sacred love. It also was another kind of invitation—an invitation to play and be a child and have fun!

****

A man came to a sadhu and asked the sadhu to make him a sadhu. The sadhu's reply was simple. He said, "First you must learn to be a thief and a baby."

The Mahatma then explained that there are things we can learn from a thief. A thief, for example, always works at night. (By this time in the story, Jnananandaji was beginning to wear one of His lustrous, yet slightly mischievous, smiles!)

Thieves work in silence. They do not tell people what they do.

"A thief," the Mahatma continued, "loves the company of other thieves, and he will NEVER change his profession. And if he fails, he tries again."

From a baby, learn to weep, laugh, and stay busy all the time.

****

One day Sumakshi and I had gone to a store in Dehradun to buy two copies of Maharaj's book, with the intention to give one away as a gift. When we arrived at satsang, we mentioned that we had been able to find the book and Maharaj exclaimed, "Oh! You found it! He had them! Maybe I should buy some copies of my book. Why not?"

What a joy! We had no exact plans as to who to give the book to, so we were able to gift it to Sri Jnananandaji Himself.

That day, we had taken two yellow flowers from the walk and Sumakshi put them in the book just before we gave it to Him.

It was fitting, because once when the Mahatma had given a book of poems to Sumakshi, He also gave her a yellow flower and He gave one to me—two flowers and a book. The flowers that He had given us were the exact same kind we had picked and placed in the book today, even though we did not know we would be gifting the book to Him! Love has a magical way of finding its way back to the source.

✳✳✳✳✳✳✳✳✳✳✳✳✳✳✳✳✳

One night in satsang, Jnananandaji mentioned that there are three kinds of happiness: original, great (maha) and supreme (param). "Steve almost had supreme joy during the chant today! He was almost levitating. It is dangerous to come here! Come at our own risk." He laughed with great joy, clapping His hands together.

For me, truly there was no greater joy than to be in His Presence.

✳✳✳✳✳✳✳✳✳✳✳✳✳✳✳✳

One day, Sumakshi and I went in search of the place which the Mahatma called one of the wonders of India: an old building with three doors that held a deep attraction for the Mahatma, who said that it was an excellent place for chanting Sanskrit mantras.

When we got there, all three doors were locked, but we managed to walk around the building and climb in through an open window. When Jnananandaji heard we had climbed through the window, He said, "I had not asked you to do that but I had thought it, and you caught my thought. Well done! Very well done!"

A moment later, referring to the adventure, He asked "How did you do it? It needs some acrobatic skills... but you are yogis," He said with a big smile, "you are fit."

✳✳✳✳✳✳✳✳✳✳✳✳✳✳✳✳✳

The Mahatma was walking one day and saw a dead cow on the side of the road in a ravine. The next day, He returned to the site with a little Ganges water, but the body of the cow had been removed. The Mahatma talked to the school authorities about it, and even asked at the Cantonment board.

"The reason I wanted to put Gangajal on the cow," Jnananandaji said, "is that even if the animal is dead, sometimes the soul still hasn't left the body. It takes a little time. Shankarcharya said if you drink even one drop of the Ganges, it has put you on the path to immortality. It is that powerful."

The Mahatma had water from Mount Kailash, Mansarovar, Gangeshwaram, Rameshwarm, and some other places.

The Mahatma showed amazing love for all beings, including those who had already left for another plane.

✳✳✳✳✳✳✳✳✳✳✳✳✳✳✳✳✳

One day, the Mahatma was talking about Chandra Swami, who was a mauni.[82] The Mahatma's simple comment to someone who was on their way to see him was, "Be polite. Talk if he talks, write if he writes, and be silent if he is silent. It is polite... don't you think

---

[82] A mauni is one who does not speak, or one who maintains holy silence at least with the spoken word.

so? If I meet a deaf and dumb man on the street I won't talk, I would use sign language."

Once, the Brahmhacharis of Dakshineswar had decided to keep silence. Only the Guru talked. After a few days He said, "I can't stand this! It sounds like a deaf and dumb school!"

For the Mahatma, everything had its own season and rhythm. Silence, of course, was golden, but He knew also how to inspire us with words and stories.

At Dakshineswar outside Kolkata
(From left: Devendra, Jemal, Steve, Jaidhara)

****

There was a saint once that spent much of his time in silence, he had just a few disciples. (Mahatmaji made a sort of gesture here that implied that the ways of God and saints are strange indeed.)

The disciples came to the saint and said there was a group of about 100 people that wanted to hear the saint give a talk. The saint said, "It is useless." Still, the devotees kept asking, and so, finally, the saint said okay, and the meeting was set for Sunday.

Then the group was all gathered together, and they sat the saint up on the dais, and he said, "Do you know the subject of my lecture?" The crowd looked at one another and then replied, "No."

"Then it is no use," the saint said, and he walked out of the room.

Still, the close disciples came and said, "Oh sir, these people very much want your blessing, you must try again." And the saint said, "It is useless," but the disciples kept asking, and so, finally, he agreed.

This time, of course, they knew what they were going to answer if he asked that question, and indeed the saint did come, and he sat again on the dais, and he said, "Do you know what I am going to talk about?"

"Yes," the people replied, confidently.

"Then there is no need to give the talk," the saint replied, and he walked out a second time.

The disciples just kept asking though, saying the people really wanted to see him talk, and so finally he agreed to talk for a third time.

"Do you know what my topic is?" the saint asked.

"Some of us know," the people replied, "and some of us do not know."

★★★★★★★★★★★★★★★★★

During this visit, Maharaj commented more about technology than usual, even the technology that floats in outer space.

"Solar and lunar eclipses," He said, "are controlled by demons."

When He was a sadhu in Haradwar, they used to take a bath before the eclipse, during the eclipse, and then again after the eclipse.

Additionally, no food was to be taken during the eclipse, or even laid out for preparation during the eclipse.

"Nowadays, there are thousands of things circling the earth. Planes, satellites—there are thousands! Imagine! Thousands of little partial eclipses happening all the time.

It says in the scriptures of India that the next incarnation of Vishnu is Kalki Avatar, and that He comes from the sky on a white horse. This is technology, and it is already here."

Some devotees pressed Maharaj about the state of affairs and He said, "Yes, just a few days left."

In a somewhat worried tone, one of the disciples said, "How many days, Sir?"

To which Maharaj gave one of His more curious answers, that "as long as there is prasad, it will be alright."

He also mentioned that in German, the word "kaput" means "broken," or that something does not work. Then He mentioned that that sound starts the word "computer." In Hindi, the same word means "bad boy." When translated for Him, Maharaj asked if there was such a word that means "bad girl," and everyone said no, there was no such word in Hindi.

When Maharaj heard that, He smiled and said, "Yes, it is the bad boy that will mis-use the computer. Of course it is okay to use these things," He added, "but one must be careful."

****

Maharaj told the story tonight of meeting Markandeya Rishi, who was the favorite deva of Maharaj. This was the deva that had seen the advent of Ram 20 times, and the advent of Sri Krishna 15 times. This deva was mostly in deep meditation, in the trance state, but would come out occasionally and see these things.

Sri Jnanandaji often tells this story of a time in old India where there used to be a gathering of devas in the mountains, and only Himself and a few other westerners were privy to this.

At that special event, a priest would answer questions on behalf of the devas. And Maharaj, in His mind, asked that deva, "Have I been always with you forever?" And the answer came back, "Yes."

"The devas of the mountains have powers," Maharaj added. "They can make it rain, or they can withhold rain. They keep this power to themselves, though, otherwise people would misuse it."

****

Maharaj had a visitor from Germany, one Reinhold. It was the first time I ever heard Maharaj really speak German-Swiss.

During that satsang, Maharaj said when He was a child in school, they had written on the board, "Don't be angry." This reminder was apparently for the students to remind the teachers!

"Students are great imitators, and not only of what you say you are teaching, but of everything. In olden Switzerland, if teachers were drinking or smoking, they would be thrown out of the school. They were there to set an example in every way."

Maharaj mentioned several other older customs which had been forgotten. He said in the India of old, you would not clear the dishes before everyone was done eating and drinking. Interestingly, this was true even in my childhood in America.

According to the Mahatma, a much worse modern habit is that of eating while standing. "Sri Pad Baba forbade it in His presence. It is bad for the health."

✳✳✳✳✳✳✳✳✳✳✳✳✳✳✳✳✳

One day, Maharaj got talking on the subject of relationships, and, as usual, some wonderful inspirations came.

Maharaj had often said that one plus one equals 11. It was His simple way of saying that if two people were in harmony, the energy was much greater than the sum of those two people.

On the other hand, He added today that if the two people are out of harmony, then the energy goes to a third—meaning that the energy goes to a third party. "It can be anyone," He said, "like a lawyer, or the court, or another person."

Mahatmaji then added that He was once speaking with Krishnanandaji, and Krishnanandaji said that if someone insults you, and you take it calmly, then your disease goes to them. So even the disharmony of disease can be overcome if one remains neutral. The last sentence the Mahatmaji said on this subject: "You must never be critical."

When looking at disharmony there are many ways to see it. The Mahatma had an amazing way of saying the word "pro-blem" as if the accent was on the "pro" which somehow made even the word "problem" sweet! Still, He mentioned the following list of ways to see a pro-blem:

    1) I have a problem.
    2) We have a problem.
    3) There is a problem.
    4) You are the problem.

He did not comment further on the matter, but it seems that if you get to number four, then you really have a problem!

✶✶✶✶✶✶✶✶✶✶✶✶✶✶✶✶

Maharaj was, of course, very fond of prasad, and He often would tell us about the benefits of prasad.

"Don't tell anyone how much prasad you get when you come here," He would say comically, "Otherwise the whole neighborhood will be here for satsang!"

As I mentioned before, He would often joke about prasad and concentration, but, somehow, as He told it tonight, I heard it differently. He was comparing prasad to grace, and saying that so much grace comes.

Then, with a smile, He was talking about the concentration that comes with prasad, and He said, "You see, when prasad comes, you forget everything."

And I understood, He was talking about samadhi. When ecstasy comes, everything else goes, even the sense you have of who you are.

****

Some kriya yogis came to satsang tonight with some specific questions about kriya. They were having some odd experiences with the kundalini energy, and they wanted to ask the saint for clarification.

Maharaj's answer was direct and simple, "Who gave you kriya? Who gave you kriya is your Guru. You should ask them."

"The Guru takes responsibility for the physical, mental, and spiritual well-being of the disciple. He takes full responsibility."

In the case of these yogis, their Guru had left the body, and they did not feel there was anyone left in their tradition who could answer the question.

"If they cannot answer the question," He said, "Then they should not be giving initiation."

He added that someone who initiates people into kriya must be able to control not only his own life force, but the life force in those that he initiates.

****

"Women are the greatest force on this earth,"
Mahatmaji said one night with a smile.

"The catholic prayer is our Father which art in heaven.
The woman is of the earth."

That is why when Mukunda was asked, "Where is
Swamiji from?" He answered "Akash," or space.
Swami is from heaven![83]

****

Tonight, Sri Maharaj told the story He often told
about the thief and the baby (told earlier) which ends
with the fact that a sadhu should be like a baby who
should "laugh, cry, and be busy all the time."

Then He added something fascinating:

"Most people," He said, "have forgotten how to laugh
in an original way, and neither can they cry in an
original way. They laugh when other people laugh,
and cry when other people cry."

This was a revelation.

We even cry as copies.

It brings new light to origin-ality.

---

[83] In *Transcendent Journey*, a young Mukunda is being carried by Sri
Jnananandaji, and they come upon a stranger that thinks the Maharaj is
kidnapping the child. So the man asks where Maharaj is from, and
Mukunda answers "Swamiji is from the akash." Then the man asks
where Mukunda is from, and the little boy answers, "Mukunda is from
Girnar." Girnar is the sacred mountain of Shiva in Gujarat, India.

****

When Maharaj was staying at Panna with the royal family, they used to have big events and sing.

At that time, there were bands of dacoits,[84] but they were not normal dacoits—they were extremely organized. They were, for example, quite loyal to the king and the royal family, and even in their own ranks there was a definite hierarchy.

Furthermore, they were, in a certain sense, a kind of police. Maharaj said that they never hurt people who were doing good and kind things and had good ways.

The head of the dacoits was a musician, and once, on Shivaratri,[85] he and Maharaj were elbow-to-elbow chanting and playing music together. Maharaj asked the princess of Panna quietly, "How many people has this man killed?"

It is a strange world, indeed. Still, the man must have had some good karma to be singing next to one of the great saints of India!

****

Tonight, Maharaj was revisiting the story about the Princess who had a Bengali guru who had given her the paper that said, "Be love," which she had kept next to her heart for many years. He mentioned that, when it came up, He was teaching them the first four steps of Vedanta, which are as follows:

---

[84] Dacoits are thieves.

[85] Shivaratri is an all-night celebration of Shiva that is celebrated once per year as Maha Shivaratri.

1) Listen. But this is misunderstood, and taken to mean "listen to talks" or "listen to books." It means to listen to the Guru mantra.
2) Think.
3) Meditate.
4) Become.

Then He simply said, "You can apply that to love."

First you hear about love, and then you think about love, and then you are in love, and then you become love.

Love is perhaps one of the greatest teachers of all.

****

In the satsang room of Maharaj, there were several statues that were quite beautiful. There was thinking Ganesh, Nandi, and then Ganesh crawling and eating a ladu.

Tonight, Maharaj mentioned something completely new, that those statues represent stages of the soul's journey.

Ganesh is thinking, with his left hand on the cheek, activating the spiritual side of the brain.

Nandi is past thought, he is no longer thinking.

Kneeling Ganesh is enjoying the sweet fruits of not thinking.

In this stage of life the Maharaj was starting to withdraw a little from the world. "Talking is copper,"

Maharaj said that day, "and the price of copper is rising... the time is close."

Though I think it is in Maharaj's book, He outlined more clearly for me the stages of spiritual evolution represented in His song Ananda Mayuum.

The stages in the song are: "Ananda mayuum, Krishna mayuum, Gopala mayuum, Shiva shanti mayuum, and Brahma mayuum," and He went on to describe them one by one.

Ananda... You feel the bliss of your own heart.

That leads you to the godhead, Krishna, but it is still impersonal.

Then Gopala... Now it is personal.[86]

Shiva shanti... Shiva drowns the little self. The destruction is complete.

Brahma... All is recognized as the One.

****

At the end of the satsang today, Mahatmaji commented, "All the birds are flying away!"

---

[86] Gopala is the infant form of Krishna. More sweet and more personal.

Maharaj

ACKNOWLEDGEMENTS

To my wonderful editor and friend Cayla Dickenson, whose help and support were invaluable.

Many of the photos in the book were taken from the beautiful work of Radheshwari. Please take a look at her website, https://radheshwari.blogspot.com/, or her YouTube channel, https://www.youtube.com/@RadhemaRadheshwari.

Printed in Great Britain
by Amazon